BEHIND ENEMY LINES:

A Discipleship Course in Spiritual Warfare
Revised and Expanded 2nd Edition

Mark and Dallas Henslee

Published by
Blue Fire Legacy
Westcliffe, Colorado

Unless otherwise indicated, all Scripture quotations are from the ESV® Bible (The Holy Bible, English Standard Version®), copyright © 2001 by Crossway, a publishing ministry of Good News Publishers. Used by permission. All rights reserved.

Other versions used are:
NASB--Scripture taken from the NEW AMERICAN STANDARD BIBLE®, Copyright © 1960, 1962, 1963, 1968, 1971, 1972, 1973, 1975, 1977, 1995 by the Lockman Foundation. Used by permission. www.Lockman.org.
NIV--THE HOLY BIBLE, NEW INTERNATIONAL VERSION®, NIV® Copyright © 1973, 1978, 1984, 2011 by Biblica, Inc.™ Used by permission. All rights reserved worldwide.
NKJV--Scripture taken from the New King James Version®. Copyright © 1982 by Thomas Nelson. Used by permission. All rights reserved.
TPT--Scripture quotations marked TPT are taken from *The Psalms: Poetry on Fire, The Passion Translation®,* copyright ©2014. Used by permission of BroadStreet Publishing Group, LLC, Racine, Wisconsin, USA. All rights reserved.

All works cited in the bibliography are used with permission. All rights reserved.

To protect the privacy of individuals whose stories are told in this book, permission has been obtained to share the stories or names have been fictionalized, although they are based on historic events.

© 2017 and 2019 Mark and Dallas Henslee

Cover Design by Dallas Henslee
Interior Graphic Design by Danielle Henslee

ISBN 978-0-9989548-1-3

All rights reserved. No part of this book may be reproduced, stored in a retrieval system, or transmitted in any form or by any means—electronic, mechanical, photocopy, recording, or otherwise—without prior written permission of the copyright owner. Please direct your inquiries to info@bluefirelegacy.org.

TABLE OF CONTENTS

Acknowledgments v
Disclaimers vii
Preface ix
Introduction xi
Prayer xvii
What is Spiritual Warfare? 19
Salvation 25
The Armor of God 35
Baptism 51
Forgiveness 67
Doors, Legal Rights, and Strongholds 87
Believers Authority in Christ 101
Protection after the Battle 111
Weapons and Techniques of Warfare 117
How Satan Works 139
The Players and Specific Spirits 157
Walking in Victory 167
Appendix 175
    Letter on Commanding 177
    Why Flags 181
    Questions and Answers 189
    In Defense of a Warfare Worldview 209
    Leader's Guide 229
Bibliography 235

ACKNOWLEDGMENTS

We are so grateful to those who have come alongside us throughout the duration and expansion of this project. This book is a compilation of what we have gleaned through Scripture and have learned over the years from many individuals and experiences. Additional thanks are extended to those who have mentored us and those who have given us the privilege of working with them. Ultimately, the Lord is to receive all the honor and glory.

DISCLAIMERS

Many resources and quotes are provided throughout the material. Just because we quote someone or provide information on material they have written or produced does not mean that we endorse or are necessarily in total agreement with all of their works, ideas, and ideologies. You may find that you disagree with some of our positions. We are simply sharing what we have learned to this point, and we recognize that, as we grow in Christ, our understanding continues to deepen. It is very important, even with our material, that you compare all teaching to the Word of God, the Holy Bible.

Reading this material can cause abreactions (side-effects). Those choosing to read our book have done so willingly with the understanding that the intensity of the material being discussed may cause any of the following:

* Conviction of the Holy Spirit
* New perceptions of the Kingdom of God
* New perceptions of your role as a Believer
* It may "ruin" church for you by creating a desire for more. (Don't say you weren't warned.)
* Manifestations of the Holy Spirit, as well as angelic and demonic spirits.

PREFACE

Sometimes, we wonder how people will react to the materials we are teaching. This curiosity comes with an understanding of the skeptics, because we were once included among you. Please understand that we are not offended by your questions and earnest seeking. We desire that you come to know even more fully the character and presence of our God who is the same yesterday, today, and tomorrow for all eternity (Hebrews 13:8).

It is our conviction that God still works miraculously today just as He did in the Bible, and He desires to include His children in the ministering process. We've heard of miracles that fall more into a category of mysterious, and wonder, like some of you, why God would choose to do things in that manner. Personally, we feel if God wants to do it that way, we shouldn't waste time wondering why.

We also want to emphasize that not everything in life is the result of a spirit or demon. Some things are just physical or are the result of an individual's choices. It is important to understand how the spirit realm works and the principles of spiritual warfare. However, it should never become more important than our relationship with Jesus Christ. Our primary focus should always be Christ. Engaging in spiritual warfare is to be an act of obedience when the Lord instructs us to engage.

As you read and learn, you may notice that the material has been written by both of us together. This means that there will be times when Mark's voice is prevalent and other times when Dallas' writing style will show through. We have provided examples of God working and lessons we have learned from our individual perspectives.

We have found it necessary to expound on some of the material as presented in the first edition to further clarify in some areas and to be more complete in the presentation in others. Questions that we have received and their answers have been added to the appendix.

Our prayer for you as you study, learn, and seek Him is that you too will come to a place of incredible awe of the one true God of the universe. We also pray that you will participate in what He is choosing to do in and through people who are submitted to His will; and furthermore, that your life will **never** again be the same.

INTRODUCTION

We were meeting with two of our pastors for lunch, and as we discussed our lives, one of them said, "Now, wait. How in the world do two Southern Baptist kids wind up here?" Her amazement was based on the fact that we believe all of the gifts exist today, that Christians are to actively engage in spiritual warfare, and that we have participated in signs and wonders given in the way of miraculous healings to those with whom God had a divine appointment.

The short answer is that God continues to reveal more of Who He is and has asked us to journey with Him after making Him Lord of our lives. The slightly longer answer is that God has been calling us into this place of ministry over a long period of time. That means we surrendered everything to Him, and He has grown our faith as we follow where He leads. Surrendering everything meant leaving family and friends, starting over in a new location (more than once), giving up preconceived notions of our identity and professions, capturing our thoughts and making them align with Christ's Truth, and loving everyone, even the seemingly "unlovable."

Dallas: I recall listening with my dad to Bob Larson on the radio while I waited with him to pick up my mom from the middle school where she taught. Outside of listening to the program (and not being sure if it was okay to agree with everything he was teaching, because it didn't fit in the Southern Baptist box), I really didn't have much exposure to deliverance and inner healing until much later.

That being said, during our younger married years, we were blessed to belong to a church that believed in passionate worship and embraced the concept that every member is a minister, meaning we prayed with each other at any point in the service as the Spirit directed. Sometimes it was two people at the altar, and sometimes we prayed corporately as a body of Believers for an individual.

Mark: As a teenager, I didn't ever really fit into the church youth group or any other group of kids my age. God had set me apart and placed a calling for ministry on my life at an early age. In 1983, after much rebellion and fighting, I surrendered my life to that call. Looking back, I can say that I had no clue what God had in store, and I am not sure even today what He has planned for the future.

Throughout my teen and college years, I struggled with what a call of God meant, as well as how I was supposed to fulfill that call. I attempted to do all the right things. I know now that God just wanted me to be available for Him to use, rather than for me to figure out how to be used and do it.

Throughout these years, I knew that there was more to being a Christian than going to church, reading the Bible, praying and doing good things. I'd been on a journey of searching and discovery for about thirty years before beginning to fully operate in the role of spiritual warrior. During those years, I would listen to music that talked about warfare, such as Petra's "This Means War," Stryper's "To Hell with the Devil," Whitecross, Rez Band and many others that were declaring war on the devil and his realm. I read books by authors such as Hal Lindsey, Bob Larson and others.

But it wasn't until I gave up on the church and "Christianity," that God completely and totally annihilated the box that I had built to contain Him. Our God is too big, too awesome, too everything to be stuck in a box of our making. If you have a box that you have God placed in, I recommend that you hand that to Him. The amazing freedom and power of His fullness in my life now is something that I wish I had discovered long ago.

****

While Dallas was attending graduate school, she had a professor who later became a close friend who taught classes, like Grief Counseling, Crisis and Trauma Counseling, and Counseling for PTSD. These were some of her favorite classes, because they represented hope and healing for those who are so wounded. Dallas' professor taught about inner healing and later suggested that she consider training in a Christian-based therapy.

These were the circumstances that God used to challenge our beliefs and man-made restrictions on His power, as well as some of the divine appointments that God set aside for Dallas to see more of Who He is. In addition, these are some of the tools that He used to heal and restore her, so she could minister to her husband and children. We became a family of spiritual warriors that continue to passionately seek after God and want to spread His love to those around us.

John Paul Jackson points out, "The enemy has always sought to silence God's prophetic voices and abort intercessory prayer. (Jackson, J. *Unmasking the Jezebel Spirit*, Pg. 2)

The enemy so wanted to abort the call God had on Mark's and Dallas' lives that each of their mothers were told they would **never** have children. God worked miracles and not only did both women have multiple children, but God brought two of those children together as helpmates and a team and taught us about spiritual warfare with a calling not only to battle but to teach others how to battle as well.

Dallas shared with Mark that when she was younger, she always wanted an exciting testimony. Of course, at the time, she didn't realize what she was asking. She realizes now that she probably should have followed that up with an apology to him that he's had to endure some of the heartache that goes into our testimony now, but she didn't think of it at the time.

While we don't have much of a story about before we were saved, we have a lot to share about what God has done in our lives, carried us through, and taught us. Here are some of the lessons He's taught us and brought us through:

* Take every thought captive. No Stinking Thinking! 2 Corinthians 10:5
* Guard your heart. Proverbs 4:23

* Faith, hope, and love remain, but the greatest of these is love. 1 Corinthians 13:13
* We fight NOT against flesh and blood, for to do so wounds people God loves. Ephesians 6:12
* He has NOT given a spirit of timidity. We have rejoiced over that in times of active warfare. 2 Timothy 1:7
* Stand firm. Sometimes, this is extremely difficult, but do it anyway. Exodus 14:13, 2 Chronicles 20:11, 1 Corinthians 16:13, Ephesians 6:13
* Walk by faith and not by sight. We believe we will walk this one out until the end of our earthly days. 2 Corinthians 5:7
* Live by and voice God's Word with fidelity; do not add or subtract. Deuteronomy 4:2; Proverbs 30:6
* God works ALL things together for His glory and for the good of those that love Him. Even when we cannot see the forest for the trees. Romans 8:28
* He goes before us and behind, directing every step. Exodus 13:21
* He has taken us through exile and has restored us from it. Jeremiah 29:10-14
* His grace is sufficient, and Christ is made strong in our weaknesses. 2 Corinthians 12:9-10
* We can overcome through Christ because greater is He in us than he in the world, and there is no fear in love. I John 4:4, 18

PRAYER

Father, we come before You and acknowledge who You are. You are the Great I Am, You and You alone are worthy of our praise. Abba, we ask that You surround us with Your presence, and that You dispel all distractions, misunderstandings, confusion, doubt, denial, and all other demonic spirits that have been assigned to this time and this place for the sole purpose of keeping Your children in the dark deception that has become all too comfortable. Right now, Lord Jesus, we acknowledge Your perfect sacrifice and victory over death. We confess that You are King of kings and Lord of lords and that our salvation and authority come only by the covering provided by Your name and shed blood. Holy Spirit send Your divine interpretations and understanding, Your power, Your conviction, and Your redeeming comfort as we study about the ultimate power struggle. We stand together and declare that while we know there is a battle raging in the heavens, You are already victorious through the shed blood and resurrection of Jesus Christ, and that this spiritual war will be terminated at a time of Your choosing, Father. Furthermore, we rejoice that You will continue to reign forever victorious.

Place on each person here Your protective armor, and Lord, provide a place of grace and extra protection for those newer in the faith and/or those who have steps of obedience that they still need to complete. We ask that You surround us and those we care about with Your angels to defend us and thwart every attempt to attack and effort to overhear the training and confessions in the hopes of strengthening the accusations Satan would hurl at us. Provide us with a grace bubble and open up a place in the heavens that prayers can pass unimpeded and without being intercepted by demonic forces.

Allow us to see each other through eyes of love and forgiveness instead of judgment. Keep us mindful of your love and mercy and grace.

Bless our time of learning. In the authority of Jesus' name, we ask that all these things be made so. Amen.

WHAT IS SPIRITUAL WARFARE?

In Matthew 16, Jesus says to Peter: "I tell you, you are Peter, and on this rock, I will build my church, and the gates of hell shall not prevail against it. I will give you the keys of the kingdom of heaven and whatever you bind on earth shall be bound in heaven, and whatever you loose on earth shall be loosed in heaven." (Matthew 16:18-19)

In Ephesians 6, Paul tells the church: "Finally, be strong in the Lord and in the strength of his might. Put on the whole armor of God, that you may be able to stand against the schemes of the devil. For we do not wrestle with flesh and blood, but against the rulers, against the authorities, against the cosmic powers over this present darkness, against the spiritual forces of evil in the heavenly places." (Ephesians 6:10-12)

These verses give us the primary definition of spiritual warfare. First, we see who is involved. Jesus spoke to Peter about His church. Paul wrote to the church at Ephesus. Spiritual warriors are the members of Christ's church. The Church, as Christ's Bride stands in unity with Him and battles against the gates of hell. Paul tells us that our battle is against evil spiritual forces.

Let's think about gates. In the physical realm, what do gates do? Gates are security devices put in place to protect, or to regulate entrance or exit. Gates do NOT go marching down the street and attack. Satan and his minions have taken territory from what is rightly ours (the Church's) and to protect that ground they have placed gates. God created the earth, and all that is in it is His (Colossians 1:16). He also created the heavens (spiritual realms). So as His children, all that belongs to Him is rightfully ours. As spiritual warriors, we are to go against these gates and break through them to reclaim the territory that has been stolen. Notice what Jesus said about our attack: "the gates of hell shall not prevail." In other words, we, the church of Jesus Christ, will be able to successfully reclaim the stolen territory.

Far too often, Christians just wait for the evil one to come against them and react when that happens. Instead, we are commanded here to go and attack the gates of hell (Luke 4:18, Mark 6:7 and Luke 10:1-3, 19-20). In other words, we are to be proactive. When Christ tells Peter that the gates of hell shall not prevail against the church, He is telling us that we need to go tear down the gates that the evil one has put in place. We are to reclaim the territory that has been taken away from the church. We are to go and free the captives from bondage. Spiritual warfare is an offensive and defensive battle.

In the battle, we need to be sure that we are battling where God wants us. If we step outside of the boundaries that God places on our activity, we are putting ourselves and those around us into harm's way. How do we know those boundaries? We must be in communication with God and hearing the Holy Spirit speak.

In Ephesians, we see a list of spiritual beings. Paul is defining our enemy. The enemy that we battle encompasses the "spiritual forces of evil." Spiritual warfare is against the powers of darkness. We will discuss in a later chapter the "lowerarchy" of the enemy.

The enemy is not stupid or naïve. Satan doesn't just arbitrarily go about harassing people and causing havoc. Paul tells us that the devil schemes. He has plans and a structure to his organization. We also need to be wise in battle with a plan that is not our own but given by the Holy Spirit. Jesus told the disciples, "Behold, I am sending you out as sheep in the midst of wolves, so be wise as serpents and innocent as doves." (Matthew 10:16)

It is important to remember when we are battling that we are not going against people, who are merely the physical hosts of the evil spirits. We have to take care to love the person as we battle to remove the spirits that have attacked them. Our objective is to break down the gates of hell and provide freedom to individuals. If we tear down or beat up the person, we are further hurting instead of helping them.

In all spiritual warfare, we *always love the people* but deal with the destruction the devil is using against them to cause defeat. When we forget that, we become agents of hurt and destruction, too.

As an example, during a deliverance session, we worked as a team to care for the person while dealing with the enemy. While Mark was addressing the spirits, the individual would look to Dallas for reassurance of their safety. It was clearly the evil spirits that Mark saw when looking in their eyes, yet when they looked at Dallas, she clearly saw the individual. It is wise to alert the individual at the beginning of the session that any sternness of voice is not directed personally at them but rather toward the residing spirits.

Jesus gives to the church the "keys to the kingdom of heaven." As we go into battle, we are not battling in our own strength and means. Spiritual warriors battle in the authority of Christ. We will be defeated if we attempt to go against evil forces in our own authority. It is only in the power and authority that the Father has bestowed upon Christ and the Holy Spirit that we are able to battle effectively. Remember the time in Acts when the sons of Sceva were trying to cast out demons (Acts 19:13-16). The demons beat them severely, because they were not strong enough without the power of God.

Our power comes through the Holy Spirit. Jesus told the disciples in Acts 1:8, "you will receive power when the Holy Spirit has come upon you."

We have been given great power to bind and to loose here on earth and in heaven. We read in Isaiah 61:1, "The Spirit of the Sovereign Lord is on me, because the Lord has anointed me to preach good news to the poor. He has sent me to bind up the brokenhearted, to proclaim freedom for the captives and release from darkness for the prisoners (NIV)."

In the power of the Holy Spirit, we are to bind up the brokenhearted and free the prisoners from darkness. We live in a world full of brokenhearted people who have been abused and beat down by the evil one. There are millions of people being held captive in prisons of darkness without the light of Christ. Millions are being held captive by sin and curses. We are to go into battle to free these captives from the grasp of the evil one. We are to care for and provide healing for those who have been broken in body, soul, and spirit. The goal of spiritual warfare is healing.

In Ephesians 6:15 when describing the armor of God, we are told to put on the readiness of the gospel of peace. It seems odd that in talking about warfare, we are to be ready with peace, but it makes perfect sense. We don't battle because we enjoy the struggle or want the battle to continue. We battle to bring about peace.

Here is a definition of spiritual warfare: Spiritual warfare is Christ's church going against the spiritual forces of darkness in the authority and power of Christ to bring about healing and peace.

CHAPTER QUESTIONS

* Do you feel more drawn to offensive or defensive battles? Why?

* Have you ever experienced defeat trying to battle in your own strength rather than in Christ's? How would you approach a similar situation differently now?

SALVATION

Salvation places a seal on the Believer. Because God is perfect and does not sin or find pleasure in sinful behavior, once you invite the Holy Spirit to reside in your spirit, it is completely secure and cannot be possessed or infiltrated by demonic beings (Ephesians 1:13, 2 Timothy 2:21).

Richard Ing says, "Others claim that when we become Christians, we are cleansed of all demons. The Bible does not say that. It says that our sins are washed away by the blood, but does not mention demons. It is true, however, that demons cannot 'possess' us [Christians]" (Ing, R. *Spiritual Warfare,* Pg. 13, brackets added).

We believe that Believers cannot be demon possessed; however, we can be influenced by demons. Possession indicates ownership, while influence allows an effect on the person but not ownership. We do ***not*** believe that Christians can be possessed (owned) by a demon though non-believers can. The Father of Lies is continually attempting to get us to believe false thoughts. We are often easily distracted and too often believe the enemy's lies (See also Ephesians 5:26-27, Romans 7:17-25).

Salvation provides atonement for our sin. The gift extended on the cross when Christ gave His life as a perfect sacrifice did not automatically change all our sin to acceptable behavior. Rather, it atoned for the inappropriate, disallowed, sinful behaviors, so that we could be seen by God through the Blood of Christ as having no blemish (Colossians 1:21-22, Hebrews 9:12-14, 10:10, 1 Peter 1:18-20). There are still consequences for choosing to live in sinful behavior. The only consequence God has promised to remove is that of eternal death for those that have accepted Christ as Lord and Savior of their lives. There are times when He chooses to lessen or remove consequences out of His mercy and grace, and there are other times when permitting a consequence serves as discipline for those He loves.

God provided a way for sinful humans (for ALL have sinned, Romans 3:23) to be reconciled with Him for eternity. Dr. Todd Hudnall summarizes the process this way:

When you choose to accept Christ's salvation:
* You are forgiven and pardoned of all sin (Col. 2:13).
* You are free from shame, guilt, and condemnation (Rom. 8:1).
* You are declared the righteousness of God in Christ (2 Cor. 5:21).

- You are accepted by God as if you were Jesus (Eph. 1:6).
- You can't add anything to Christ's work, but you can receive it (Eph. 8-9).

(Hudnall, T. *Because of God's Scandalous Grace*, sermon 1/12/14)

Salvation is an individual and personal decision. No one can make that choice for you. When someone gives you a gift, you have the option to receive that gift or not. You can accept the nicely wrapped box, take it home and put it on a shelf or in the closet without ever opening it. But to truly receive the gift, you need to open it and put the item into use. When you choose to receive the gift of salvation, God washes your heart whiter than snow removing all sin that has occurred prior to that point in your life.

If you have not yet made this decision, you can pray right now to receive salvation through Christ. A sample prayer can be "Jesus, I acknowledge that I am a sinner and ask that you forgive me of my sins. I desire that you be Lord of my life. Please wash me with your blood and cleanse me from all unrighteousness. I accept your gift and commit my life to you. Amen."

Salvation does not terminate all prior spiritual bonds. "Wait—when you got saved, didn't that erase those legal rights? Didn't all your sins get washed away? Wasn't that a fresh start? No, it was not an automatic clean slate. Becoming a Christian did save your soul,* and it brought you into a right relationship with Jesus Christ. But if you ever engaged the enemy in some way, even informally, that agreement remains in force over the circumstances of your life until you do something about it. You will still go to Heaven. You haven't sold your soul to the devil. But your feet will be entangled, and your life-journey will be filled with detours. Your destiny will always remain out of your grasp. You want to disentangle yourself as soon as possible, so that you can get on the winning track toward your destiny." (Larson, B. *Demon Proofing Prayers*, Pg. 33).

*Some teach there is only a distinction between body and soul rather than agreeing with the teaching that we are a tripartite being. Larson differs from our position of separating body, soul, and spirit as this quote is written. For clarity, we contend that becoming a Christian and accepting Christ as your Savior saves your *spirit,* yet the soul must still be brought into submission by allowing Christ to also be Lord of our thoughts and decisions.

For the purposes of this work, we need to define our definition of tripartite (or trichotomous) versus dichotomous beings. There is debate whether man is dichotomous - body and soul/spirit (soul and spirit being interchangeable words), or trichotomous - having body, soul, and spirit each with a separate function. The debate is beyond the scope of this work, and regardless of which side one lands on, should not result in an inability to proceed in our teaching.

Clearly, humans have a material and immaterial aspect to our being. The body is the material component of man. Many who argue a dichotomous being, differentiate the immaterial between the Greek words *psuche* (psyche) and *pneuma* which, contrary to their argument, results in the same result as our definition of trichotomous given that dividing 1 of 2 parts into parts yet again gives you 3 parts. Others argue that the soul refers to the whole being to include the body and spirit. For more of a discussion on this topic see pages 225-226.

Let's look at this in diagram form (See Body, Soul, and Spirit charts). We are a tripartite being. We have a physical body; a soul which includes our emotions, will, and mind, represented by the outer shirt area; and a spirit, represented by the inner area. The spirit portion of our being is eternal in nature.

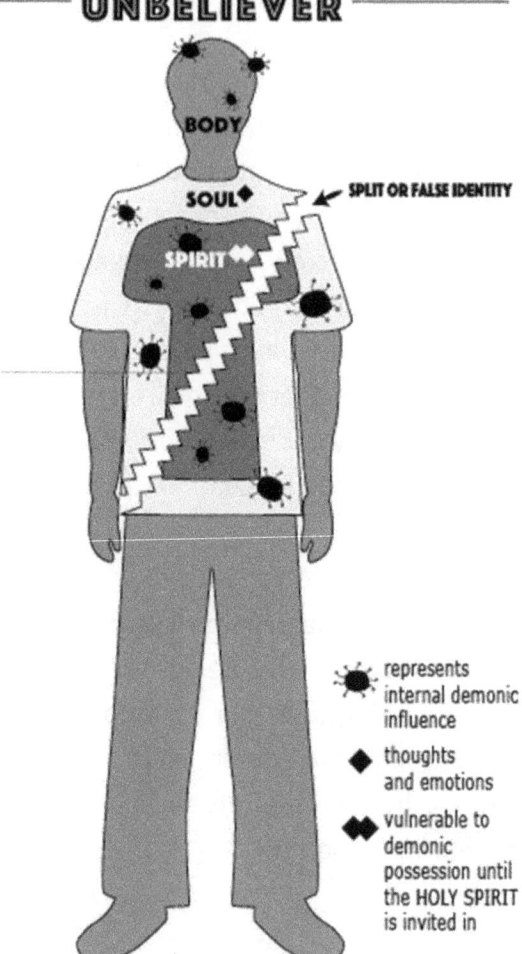

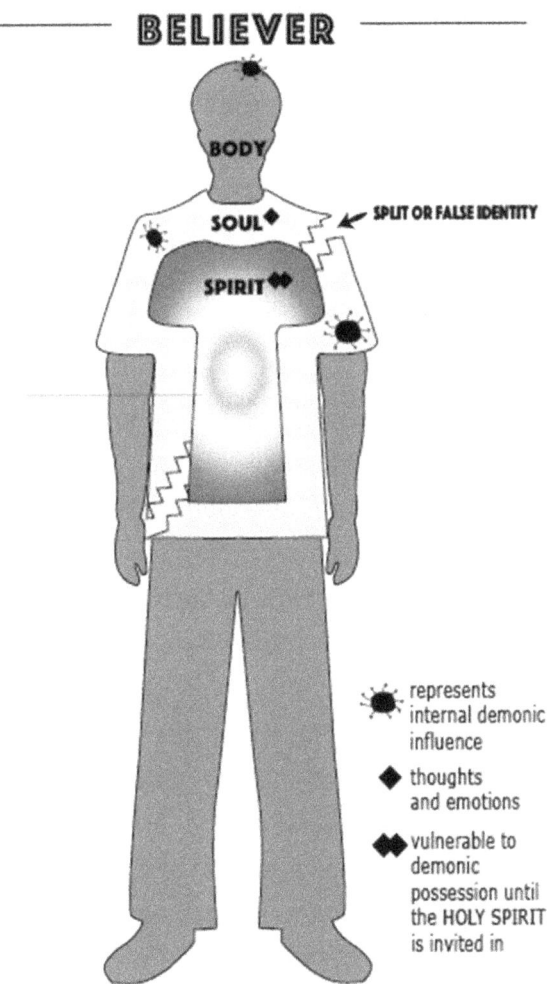

Graphics designed by Danielle Henslee

As an unbeliever, one's state prior to receiving the gift of salvation is such that demonic influences can be present in all three parts of one's being. This means that in such a state, demonic possession is possible. We were created to have a relationship with our Creator, God, which the enemy has distorted by undermining the desire for that relationship; and therefore, our identity causing a spiritual split or false identity. Furthermore, without the redemption of Christ's blood, one's spirit is vulnerable as it remains unprotected.

In contrast, as a Believer, one having made Christ the Lord of their life, the influence of the demonic is greatly diminished. The split or false identity can no longer impact one's spirit, because it is protected and sealed by the blood of Christ shed as the Perfect Sacrifice once and for all. Therefore, a split or false identity can only materialize, or manifest, in the soul (emotions, thoughts, will) and physical body. While demonic influences are not completely negated during our time on the earth, internal influences are more easily defeated in the power of Jesus' name through forgiveness and rejection of anything unholy in the form of repentance and disavowing. External demonic influences may still be assigned to Christians. The enemy doesn't give up fighting just because you made a profession of faith. (John 10:10)

When we encounter a situation that appears to be demonic, we will pray for direction from the Lord about how to proceed. We will determine the individual's relationship with Jesus Christ prior to any deliverance work. If the individual does not have the Holy Spirit, then we will discuss salvation with them before proceeding. Without the protection of the Holy Spirit living in them, we are likely not going to be able to bring about complete freedom and have the risk of leaving the person in a worse state (Luke 11:24-26).

CHAPTER QUESTIONS

* Describe your salvation experience.

* What bonds do you still need freedom from?

THE ARMOR OF GOD

Before we go into battle, we need to be prepared for what the enemy may throw our way. A key aspect of preparation is to get dressed appropriately. This means that we must put on the Armor of God as described in Ephesians 6.

Think about football players. Before they go onto the field for a game, they put on every component of their uniform, including the appropriate pads, braces, and other protective items. This is not something that they do only once in their lifetime or even once in a season. They get dressed appropriately before every game.

Likewise, we need to get dressed appropriately before every battle; however, unlike a scheduled football rival, we don't generally know ahead of time when the battle will be waged. To always be prepared, we get dressed in the armor every day. There are times when we need to redress during the day if the battle has been strong and/or wearisome.

Read Ephesians 6:10-18.

> Finally, be strong in the Lord and in the strength of His might. Put on the whole armor of God, that you may be able to stand against the schemes of the devil. For we do not wrestle against flesh and blood, but against the rulers, against the authorities, against the cosmic powers over this present darkness, against the spiritual forces of evil in the heavenly places. Therefore, take up the whole armor of God, that you may be able to withstand in the evil day, and having done all, to stand firm. Stand therefore, having fastened on the belt of truth, and having put on the breastplate of righteousness, and, as shoes for your feet, having put on the readiness given by the gospel of peace. In all circumstances take up the shield of faith, with which you can extinguish all the flaming darts of the evil one; and take the helmet of salvation, and the sword of the Spirit, which is the word of God, praying at all times in the Spirit, with all prayer and supplication. To that end keep alert with all perseverance, making supplication for all the saints.

The first thing we see is that our strength for battle comes from the Lord, and it is in His power that we fight. If you ever find yourself in a position thinking that you don't need the Lord on this one, be prepared for a humiliating defeat. If you want an example, look at Joshua 7 or 1 Samuel 4.

As we have discussed, our battle is not against flesh and blood, and therefore, our armor is not physical. It does, however, have some comparison to physical armor. Roman soldiers were outfitted in varying outfits of armor. The deciding factor was your rank, because as the armor improved in protective aspects, it became more expensive. When we look at the passage in Ephesians 6 that describes our armor, it is layered and elaborate.

We have found that God personalizes our Armor. Think again about the football team. Each player has some different types of pads and braces depending on their respective positions. A lineman wears knee braces and heavier padding, while a quarterback has smaller pads.

Remember also in 1 Samuel 17:38-39, David couldn't wear Saul's armor when he marched out to meet Goliath, because it was too heavy and was not fitted to David. While there are standard pieces of spiritual armor, God knows if there is an added vulnerability which needs to be covered; additional pieces of armor are provided to help us function as we are called into battle.

God has allowed several members of our family to see into the spirit realm what various sets of armor looks like. Dallas' armor is purple, and she has seen angels wielding burgundy shields encompass a client while praying and hearing the command, "Shields up!" Mark saw a piece of one of our daughter's armor that had pink feathers coming out of the helmet, which she later confirmed that she too has seen. Our eldest daughter was not able to see hers, but God showed Dallas that it has colorful streamers that attach on the shoulders. That seems fitting, since she is a dancer and loves the performing and visual arts. The shields can be varying sizes and shapes, the helmet may be Roman, Eastern, or sport-like in shape.... It doesn't matter so much what it looks like as much as how it functions. The pieces of your armor may vary with maturity and for specific battles. God knew we would need to be able to stand against the enemy, and so He fashioned each of us an appropriate set of armor for each task.

To prepare ourselves to put on God's armor, we begin by asking the Lord to wrap us in His cloak, giving us an extra layer of protection. The cloak embodies the power of the shed blood of Christ for us (1 Corinthians 1:30-31). God sees us as blameless through the blood of His Son, and the demons tremble at the thought of being in His presence. It is our prayer that the cloak of Christ also permits others to see Jesus shine through us as we interact daily with them.

A garment of praise is effective in warfare. Praise weakens the enemy. Throwing off a garment or attitude of heaviness can be difficult, but we encourage you to be deliberate in choosing praise regardless of the circumstances (Isaiah 61:3).

****

Now let's take a look at the different pieces of armor mentioned in Ephesians 6.

THE BELT OF TRUTH

Jesus himself said that He is The Truth (John 14:6, "Jesus said to him, 'I am the way and the truth and the life.'"). Satan is the father of lies; we must know the Truth to be able to defend against lies. Lies can come in the form of agreeing with Satan's deception and falsehoods, lying to ourselves, participating in the rumor mill about others, or believing false teachers without comparing the concepts to the Word of God.

The Truth is found by knowing the Word of God, which means we need to spend time reading and studying the Bible. Bankers are trained to know the difference between authentic and fake bills by studying the real thing rather than by studying all the potential ways to counterfeit. By knowing the look and feel of the real bill in every detail possible, they are better able to discern when a bill is counterfeit. Likewise, we need to know the real Word of God in every detail, so when it is twisted, we can recognize the deception.

We often come across opportunities to stretch the truth or benefit by remaining silent. For example, Mark went to purchase an item which didn't have a tag for scanning. The cashier asked how much the item was, and Mark couldn't remember at first if it was $2.99 or $4.99. The cashier said, "Well, you want it to be $2.99," but then Mark remembered that he had picked the more expensive item and corrected the price. The next day he was purchasing a pizza, and the cashier gave him the correct change; however, a couple minutes later, after being distracted, she came back and tried to give him more cash back. We will be tested, and God desires that we respond in truth even if it is not to our earthly benefit.

As a physical belt helps to bind together our clothing, the belt of truth binds together our armor. A soldier's belt was also important in that it was an attachment point for various tools and items needed. Similar to a fanny pack, the soldier's belt had a place for storing and carrying important items. Mark also thinks of this in the context of a workman's tool belt. He has pouches and places for the tools that he needs close and ready while working. Our spiritual belt carries the tools we need close at hand when in battle.

THE BREASTPLATE OF RIGHTEOUSNESS

We aren't able to bring righteousness to the table, because in our human nature we are all sinners. God supplies the righteousness that provides protection over our hearts and other vital organs from the front and back. Today, we might better be able to envision this piece of armor if we are to imagine putting on a bullet proof vest.

You may be wondering how the breastplate may function in battle. It is protective, because we depend on Christ's righteousness (Rom 9:30, Rom 10:4, Phil 3:9). Without Christ, the devil will have a great time accusing us when we attempt to battle without the breastplate of righteousness. In 1 Peter 5:8 we are told, "Your adversary the devil prowls around like a roaring lion, seeking someone to devour." In Zechariah 3:1 and Revelation 12:10, we are told that he is the accuser of the saints.

There have been times in our experience that we have felt the hits against our breastplate during battle. One morning while praying, a battle came forth, and Mark had not yet put on the armor that day. The enemy hit his chest and literally knocked the wind out of him. He can tell you it is hard to be commanding spirits when the wind is knocked out of you. He had to step back from the fight, regroup, get dressed appropriately and then reengage the enemy.

More than being protection from a physical hit, we need the Breastplate of Righteousness to shield us from the accusations of the enemy. When we walk in Christ's righteousness, we will have a strength beyond anything that we can physically or emotionally muster. The more we live our lives upright before the Lord, the less ammunition there is against us, and we are better able to withstand the attacks of the enemy.

THE HELMET OF SALVATION

Without salvation, an individual is just another person completely vulnerable to the blows of the devil. Believers have been redeemed by the blood of Christ, and it is in His perfect sacrifice and gift of salvation that we have any ability to stand strong.

We need to protect our thought life and be responsible to check our emotional responses through the mind of Christ. This pertains even to our sleeping hours. Ask God to consecrate your imagination and protect your dreams.

> For though we walk in the flesh, we are not waging war according to the flesh. For the weapons of our warfare are not of the flesh but have divine power to destroy strongholds. We destroy arguments and every lofty opinion raised against

the knowledge of God, and take every thought captive to obey Christ, being ready to punish every disobedience, when your obedience is complete. (2 Corinthians 10:3-6)

The helmet protects not just our thoughts but also our hearing, vision and our equilibrium. Think about what happens when you are hit in the head. If the blow is hard enough, you could suffer a concussion. Your balance can be compromised. How strong a warrior can you be if you are out of balance? So, our heads are a prime target of the enemy.

Humility is an important characteristic of a strong warrior. When we think highly of ourselves, we are more likely to suffer a fall. When we humbly focus on Christ instead of ourselves, the enemy is more easily defeated.

With the helmet of salvation, we are consecrating our physical, as well as our spiritual ears and eyes, to operate through Christ. We are claiming His protection for us to be able to hear the voice of the Holy Spirit, to discern between truths and lies spoken, and to see clearly what is occurring around us.

THE SWORD OF THE SPIRIT

Scripture is the Sword of the Spirit, God's Word, or a God Sword. Jesus modeled using the sword when He rebuked Satan with Scripture (Matthew 4 and Luke 4). Memorizing Scripture is very beneficial. The Lord will bring to mind those passages that you have memorized as they are needed. However, if you don't have a needed passage memorized, use a concordance or electronic search and read the applicable passage(s) aloud.

Scripture helps us know right from wrong, differentiate false prophets and false teachings from the truth. Scripture comforts us, encourages us, instructs us, and Scripture can be prayed and read back to God. Scripture is also a weapon against evil spirits. As Jesus was tempted and spiritually attacked by Satan in the wilderness, He responded with Scripture. Praying by reading Scripture aloud gives you another way to fight the enemy.

There was a time when Mark's personal character and business was attacked. That night in his utter distress the only way to bring any sense of relief was to read Psalm 91. We read this Psalm over and over again, in many different translations, until we could feel the peace and protection of the Father. Scripture is a mighty weapon for both offensive and defensive battle.

SHIELD OF FAITH

Faith is a crucial part of our Christian walk. God rarely allows us to know what the future holds. We rely on His character and the history of those who have gone before us to continue to believe and to exercise faith. "Faith is the assurance of things hoped for, the conviction of things not seen (Hebrews 11:1)." It is called a shield of *faith* NOT a shield of *feeling*.

When we have hope and faith, we continue to press on even during uncertainty. If you are lacking in faith, ask God to give you the supply you need.

What does your shield look like? Is it small and round? Is it wide, tall, brand new and shiny, showing signs of use with some wear and tear? Does it have holes from the enemy's fiery darts? Mark has two shields of faith and the size and shape changes depending on the battle. He can't really explain it, but he has seen a larger shield that he can stand completely behind and a smaller shield that he's able to use for defense, as well as for offense, swinging and knocking down the enemy.

We need our shields to be strong to defend against the enemy's attacks. The NASB 1977 Edition of Ephesians 6:16 says, "flaming missiles." The enemy isn't just firing toy darts or spit balls at us. He will unleash his fury, and it is important to have a strong shield to defend against his missiles. Note also that they are fiery or flaming. In the times that Scripture was written, one of the defenses used by a city was arrows that were set on fire. When the invading army (remember, we are going against the gates of hell) would attack the city gate, archers would shoot arrows from above and even if the arrow wouldn't kill, the fire would hopefully ignite the clothing or area around the invaders to disable them. This is also why Paul says "above all" in some translations as a reminder to hold your shields up, for the attack can come from all sides, including above.

Your faith will grow as you exercise it much like a muscle that is worked. If you want to have big faith, then you need to be walking in what little faith that you have now. As God works in your life through your faith, it will grow. We can look back at things that we did many years ago which we thought were huge steps of faith. Now what God is asking us to do requires so much greater faith, but we are able because we took those prior steps.

Faith requires action. James tells us that faith without works is dead (James 2:14-26). Throughout Scripture we have examples of people believing God by doing what He instructs them to do. Likewise, we must put our faith into action.

Have you ever made the statement, "I have faith that He could, **but**...?" If you follow your statement of faith with a qualifier, it isn't truly faith. Ask God to forgive you of those doubts and to repair your shield (Mark 9:24, Hebrews 11:1).

SHOES OF THE READINESS OF THE GOSPEL OF PEACE

Just as most of us don't go walking around in public barefoot, we need to put on shoes for spiritual battle. One of the characteristics of the shoes is readiness. We are to be ready for attacks of the enemy, as well as be ready to bring peace to people we encounter in our daily activities. Paul instructs Timothy to be ready in season and out of season (2 Timothy 4:2).

What is the Gospel of Peace? It is the peace of Christ that surpasses all understanding (Philippians 4:7). We are to be sharing Christ and what He has to offer to this world that is full of chaos and conflict.

Sometimes, we are called to stand strong, as Paul warns in Ephesians 6:13, "and after you have done everything, to stand." We stand in the strength of the Gospel of Christ. We must protect the integrity of the presentation of the gospel (Acts 20:27-28, Philippians 3:16). It is not that we are defending God or His Words, as He doesn't require our assistance in these areas, but rather that we are diligent in following His directives. In our churches, we need to be sure that there is not any compromise. This means taking a long look at whether we need to stop doing something that has become familiar, start doing something that we are currently neglecting, or possibly a combination of the prior two both personally and corporately.

With that in mind, we approach teaching with the maturity and understanding we have attained at any given time. We are not experts; we are simply children of the King who are still learning. If you find yourself in disagreement with our teaching or the teachings of others, we humbly suggest that you strive to develop what you believe based on Scripture rather than attacking any fellow Believer. Challenge the teaching if you feel God has directed you to do so, but remember, our best weapon in warfare is love even when applied in a situation of rebuke and reproof.

Note that we are to be ready with the gospel of peace. We talk a lot about warfare, but ultimately, God is a God of Peace. He desires that we and those to whom we minister receive peace. Ironically, we war *FOR* peace.

****

After the battle, it is important to check our equipment and repair any damage. Throughout battle our shields and other parts of our armor may become damaged.

Sometimes, we don't see a complete freedom and our faith takes a dent. We may become weary in the length of the battle and need fresh energy. It's possible that the enemy has made accusations against us during battle and we are questioning our righteousness.

It is important to ask God to reverse and correct any damage to our armor. Ultimately, He is our protection, Jehovah-Nissi, and it is by His grace that we are able to stand in the battle. He is the author and perfecter of our faith (Hebrews 12:2). He is our righteousness (Jeremiah 23:6, 33:16).

We see this as the renewal and refreshing process (Luke 9:10). We physically rest, pray, praise, worship, study Scripture, research anything new that had to be addressed in battle, seek out spiritual leaders and mentors to gain Biblical instruction, and record or journal anything of significance so that it can be referenced later, if needed. One reminder here, don't forget to date your entries.

CHAPTER QUESTIONS

* What part of the armor stands out to you the most? Why?

* Are you trying to wear someone else's armor (parent, spouse, pastor)?

* How has your armor been personalized?

BAPTISM

In this lesson, we are going to look at three baptisms. Some of you, like those who have been raised in certain churches as we were, may be thinking at this point that we've gone "off the deep end" and are teaching strange things. Bear with us and seek God's insight as we move forward.

DEFINITION OF BAPTISM

The English word "baptism" is rooted in the Greek word *baptisma* or *baptismos*. These words have the literal meaning of "to dip, immerse, wash." Figurative translations are "to overwhelm" or "to drench."

> Acts 19:1-6 And it happened that while Apollos was at Corinth, Paul passed through the inland country and came to Ephesus. There he found some disciples. And he said to them, "Did you receive the Holy Spirit when you believed?" And they said, "No, we have not even heard that there is a Holy Spirit." And he said, "Into what then were you

baptized?" They said, "Into John's baptism." And Paul said, "John baptized with the baptism of repentance, telling the people to believe in the one who was to come after him, that is, Jesus." On hearing this, they were baptized in the name of the Lord Jesus. And when Paul had laid his hands on them, the Holy Spirit came on them, and they began speaking in tongues and prophesying.

The first baptism is baptism in the blood of Christ. This occurs when we accept Christ's sacrifice and the gift of salvation. This baptism is what happens in the spiritual realm as Jesus washes one's spirit with His blood and provides forgiveness and atonement for our sins. This is referred to as being saved or born again, because it is during salvation that the Holy Spirit indwells your spirit. Again, as taught in the prior chapter, salvation is a one-time experience. You cannot fall from grace or out of being saved. If you could, it would mean Christ's sacrifice was insufficient. The Bible says Christ was the only perfect and acceptable sacrifice to move from being judged under the Law to being under grace (Ephesians 2:1-8, Titus 3:4-7, Romans 6:14).

Acts 18:18 tells us, "many of the Corinthians hearing Paul believed and were baptized." Note in this verse that there was the act of believing and then the act of baptism. As they believed, they experienced salvation. Salvation, as we previously discussed, is the first baptism, and at this point of intentional decision to give Christ Lordship of our lives, all our sins are covered (washed, drenched) by the blood of Christ.

Romans 6:3 says, "all of us who have been baptized into Christ Jesus were baptized into his death." Blood and water flowed when Christ was crucified (John 19:34). This is a good representation of the first two baptisms.

The second baptism is baptism in water. This is often called Believer's baptism and is done by immersion in water. Please remember, the water itself is not magic. Water baptism is a symbolic way of professing one's faith in Christ. Baptism by being immersed in water is a purposeful individual choice which differs from being sprinkled as an infant. In submitting to and participating in this form of baptism, one is acknowledging that Jesus, the Son of God, died on the cross for that person's sins. The act of water baptism is a public profession of your faith in Christ and your surrender to Him.

Water baptism, whether as an infant, child, or adult, is **not** the same as the gift of salvation; however, baptism initiated or requested by the individual seems to impart an additional measure of power and authority from the Holy Spirit. It is an important part of one's Christian walk. Baptism is a personal decision rather than one made on your behalf. Water baptism is a physical representation of what has occurred spiritually at the time of salvation. It is one of the ways Believers demonstrate obedience and a desire to follow the Lord in a deeper relationship with Him.

There is much symbolism in water baptism. Commonly, when baptizing, the minister (or other person performing the baptism) will say "in the likeness of Christ's death, burial and resurrection." The process of being totally submerged in the water represents several things: our death to the old man (the flesh); the burial of the old with Christ; and a washing away of our sins. As one is baptized by immersion, it depicts dying to self, sin, and human desires, and that old nature being buried. The coming up out of the water represents the hope and joy of being raised to new life in Christ just as He conquered death and rose from the grave.

> Do you not know that all of us who have been baptized into Christ Jesus were baptized into his death? We were buried therefore with him by baptism into death, in order that, just as Christ was raised from the dead by the glory of the Father, we too might walk in newness of life. Romans 6:3-4

Christ is alive today, ascended into Heaven and sitting at the right hand of the Father (Ephesians 1:20). He remains concerned with our lives and will return to call all Believers to live with Him forever in Heaven. The vessel, pool, and water used for baptism are not what convey the power. It is God and God alone Who chooses the measure of power given at the time of each baptism. Water baptism is done in the name of the Father, the Son, and the Holy Spirit, and can be repeated if the Believer feels there is reason to do so. Some reasons one might choose to be re-baptized by immersion include rededication of one's life or joining a new church family.

Water baptism is an act of obedience. When we are not in a place of obedience, the demons have a place where they can attack. This principle can be applied to other areas of our life. For example, if we are holding onto unforgiveness of another, we encourage demons to cause chaos in our thoughts, words, and actions. We will discuss that more thoroughly later.

John's baptism was more than immersion in water. It was a baptism of repentance (Matthew 3:11). He required public confession of sins (Matthew 3:6) and a life that produced fruit (Matthew 3:8). It is important that we come to God in baptism with humility, so He can do what He desires in us.

The third baptism is the baptism in the power of the Holy Spirit (Acts 1:8). This baptism does NOT provide salvation. That was complete at the time of believing in Christ (see first type of baptism above). 1 John 4:13-15 says, "This is how we know that we live in Him and He in us: He has given us of his Spirit. And we have seen and testify that the Father has sent his Son to be the Savior of the world. If anyone acknowledges that Jesus is the Son of God, God lives in them and they in God." (NIV) The key word in this passage is "acknowledges." Some translations use the word "confesses." The acknowledgement or confession that Jesus is the Son of God implies that salvation is established in the first baptism of the blood of Christ, which is the acceptance of Christ as our Lord and Savior, not in the water baptism or the baptism in the Holy Spirit.

Many churches that teach the baptism of the Holy Spirit will call themselves "Spirit-Filled" Believers or churches. All Believers are filled with the Holy Spirit at the time of salvation (John 20:22); and therefore, the Holy Spirit is present in the churches where they congregate. The difference is in the intensity, revelation, and display of the power and sensitivity to the Holy Spirit. It is also common for these groups to believe that the initial indicator of being baptized in the Holy Spirit is to speak in tongues. There are several examples in Scripture to support this belief (Acts 2:4, 10:46, 19:6); however, there are also examples of baptism in the Holy Spirit where tongues are not mentioned (e.g., Paul's baptism and filling with the Holy Spirit in Acts 9:17-19, also Acts 8:14-17). We believe that the gift of tongues is a present-day gift; however, we believe that the presence and manifestation of the *power* of the Holy Spirit can precede the physical manifestation of *any* of the spiritual gifts, including tongues.

John the Baptist said in Luke 3:16, "I baptize you with water, but He who is mightier than I is coming, the strap of whose sandals I am not worthy to untie. He will baptize you with the Holy Spirit and fire."

> Acts 1:5 Jesus said: "for John baptized with water, but you will be baptized with the Holy Spirit not many days from now."
>
> Acts 2:1-4 When the day of Pentecost arrived, they were all together in one place. And suddenly there came from heaven a sound like a mighty rushing wind, and it filled the entire house where they were sitting. And divided tongues as of fire appeared to them and rested on each one of them. And they were all filled with the Holy Spirit and began to speak in other tongues as the Spirit gave them utterance.
>
> Acts 8:14-17 Now when the apostles at Jerusalem heard that Samaria had received the word of God, they sent to them Peter and John, who came down and prayed for them that they might receive the Holy Spirit, for he had not yet fallen on any of them, but they had only been baptized in the name of the

Lord Jesus. Then they laid their hands on them and they received the Holy Spirit.

Baptism in the power of the Holy Spirit is not a one-time event. It occurs as we need it. The intensity level varies based on our need and desire for that time. Our participation in the Spirit's work is dependent on our willingness to be used how, when, and to the degree, He desires.

In each of the three types of baptism, God reveals a portion of Who He is. First, God the Father sent His Only Son to be the Savior of the world by dying on the cross in order to cover our sins through the spiritual baptism in the *blood* of Christ. Second, the saved proclaim and profess that Christ is the only way to eternal life in Heaven by an outward testimony of being baptized by *water*. Third, the Holy Spirit is asked to impart the fullness of His power in the baptism of the *Spirit*.

Christ modeled baptism for us when He asked John the Baptist to baptize Him (See Matthew 3:13; Mark 1:9). After Christ was baptized in the water, God sent the Holy Spirit like a dove to rest on Him. Many use the dove as a symbol to represent the Holy Spirit today.

Who can baptize? Every Believer is authorized to baptize in Jesus' name. It is not a requirement that it be an ordained minister.

> Then Jesus came to them and said, "All authority in heaven and on earth has been given to me. Therefore go and make disciples of all nations, baptizing them in the name of the Father and of the Son and of the Holy Spirit, and teaching them to obey everything I have commanded you. And surely I am with you always, to the very end of the age." (Matthew 28:18-20 NIV)

The Great Commission instructs us to:

1. Go
2. Make disciples
3. Baptize and
4. Teach.

With that in mind, "any Believer" changes to "all Believers" are to share in the responsibility to baptize.

****

A few testimonials on baptism:

"We had a sharp reminder recently of the importance of baptism. With a specific client, we had gathered together several times as a team to do deliverance prayer. Things had been much more difficult than we've seen before. For instance, we would command resident entities to leave in the Name of Jesus, and at times, they would recoil, but at other times they would mock us in the client's thoughts! This was seriously frustrating and confusing. Why isn't our authority in Jesus carrying the weight it should? At one point, we were taking turns reading Scripture over her and when she heard, "...repent and be baptized, every one of you for the remission of your sins..." the entities within her writhed and contorted. We noticed this and asked, "You're baptized, right?" We had just assumed all this time that she was, because she's clearly a devoted Believer and worships with a very conservative church. Well, to our amazement, she replied, "No, [I was] just sprinkled as a baby." We had been attempting to remove demonic entities based on the authority that a Believer has in Christ...the legal accomplishment of the Cross, but she wasn't fully within that covenant. Well, we promptly filled the bathroom tub and baptized her in the Name of the Father, the Son, and the Holy Spirit. We then resumed our attempt, and she was delivered within less than an hour. Now, I know there are many different views on baptism, but all I can say is that this experience reminded us that it matters. It matters to God, and it matters in deliverance. "Repent and be baptized, every one of you, in the name of Jesus Christ for the forgiveness of your sins" Acts 2:38 (*Splankna Newsletter*, December 2012).

****

Story of Christmas Baptism

We had been praying for a long time that our oldest daughter would seek Believer's baptism. She had been saved as a young child, but her numerous fears kept her from being obedient in this area of her life.

It was over a decade before she came to the place that she had enough deliverance in her life from the fear that she asked to be baptized. There were a couple of constraints, though. First, she had moved to another state to attend university, and we wanted to be present. Second, we wanted to do this with extended family present; and third, we weren't currently in leadership or even members of a church body. The first two constraints were relatively easy to work around. It was Thanksgiving when she came to the place of wanting to be baptized, and she would be home over Christmas break. Some of our extended family would also be present, as we had scheduled a ski trip together. Now, we needed a place to do the baptism.

Mark asked a friend and area pastor if we could do a private baptism in their church, and he agreed to let us do so. Great! We were all set, right? Not exactly. Because the evil spirits knew this would weaken their ability to influence our daughter, we suddenly had a huge spiritual battle with physical implications on our hands. We weren't expecting that, and, as relative novices to active spiritual warfare, we were somewhat at a loss.

Two days before the baptism was scheduled to occur, our daughter had debilitating pain in her back. Not only could she not walk or sit comfortably, but the pain was so intense that she was crying out in agony even just lying still on her bed. We prayed for deliverance and healing. We remembered the article from above that had come in a recent emailed newsletter. We can use the bathtub!

We decided to first baptize her in the bathtub in our home. She could hardly move, so Dallas was very concerned about this process. As soon as Mark reclined her into the water, there was a physical release. She came back up with relative ease. Her pain was reduced, but not entirely gone. Full healing and release came later.

Remember, part of baptism is the public nature of the profession of faith. She did report after the scheduled baptism the next day that her back was fine. Praise God. Satan's power was weakened, and she has a very vivid memory to know that God still heals. It wasn't the water or the baptistery that made the difference. It was God and God alone.

Story of Mark's Baptism in the Power of the Holy Spirit

There have been various times throughout my life that I've had the Holy Spirit come upon me in power. Most often was during sermons when the Holy Spirit would take over and preach. One example of my baptism in the Holy Spirit came in October, 2012. We had been battling a Jezebel spirit and were gathered for prayer with a group of about a dozen people. As I began to pray, the Holy Spirit came upon me in such power that it is hard to even describe. I know that the power that was flowing through me in that prayer time scared several of the people in the group. My friend had stepped outside for a minute and came back in during the Spirit's outpouring. Later, he jokingly told me that he wondered why I was yelling, but he really knew it was the Spirit coming in power against Jezebel through me.

For me it was an electrifying experience and a bit unsettling to have such power flow through me, but it was a confirmation of many things that we had been learning. This was during the time when God was annihilating the box I figuratively had built to contain Him. Another part of "the box" that I struggled with was tongues. While I had believed for many years that God still gave the gift of tongues, I typically limited that to missionaries and others ministering in foreign lands or to speakers of other languages.

As I received the power of the Holy Spirit, I wanted all that He desired to give to me. Through my intellectual processing I told Him, "God, I want all you have for me, and if that includes the gift of tongues, I'm willing. If possible, will you do so in a way that I don't freak out and think I've lost my mind?" He was more than gracious in the gifting.

The gift of tongues for me started something like a rabbinical chant. Several months later, it welled up from my heart and came out more as a song or chant than another language. The best way I can describe it is that it was a praise language to my Lord. Once I was accepting of this manner of the gift, God developed the gifting as other languages. It wasn't long before I was praying in other tongues and commanding evil spirits in languages unknown to me.

CHAPTER QUESTIONS

* How do you define baptism?

* Have you been baptized because of a personal decision?

* What is your story of baptism in the power of the Holy Spirit?

FORGIVENESS

Forgiveness is a central part of one's faith. In receiving salvation, one receives forgiveness of sin from God. While God gives salvation without requiring a set number of works or perfected obedience, there is a natural outpouring of the character of God. As we become more like Him, we will have an increased desire to forgive others for offenses committed against us.

> And whenever you stand praying, forgive, if you have anything against anyone, so that your Father also who is in heaven may forgive you your trespasses. (Mark 11:25)

> For if you forgive others their trespasses, your heavenly Father will also forgive you, but if you do not forgive others their trespasses, neither will your Father forgive your trespasses. (Matthew 6:14-15)

> Anyone whom you forgive, I also forgive. Indeed, what I have forgiven, if I have forgiven anything, has been for your sake in the presence of Christ, so that

> we would not be outwitted by Satan; for we are not ignorant of his designs. (2 Corinthians 2:10-11)

Forgiveness never implies that the act was acceptable behavior; rather it frees us from the burden of carrying around a grudge which would continue to impede our relationship with God and our witness to others. There are some wounds that are so deep that a process of inner healing will be necessary to fully expunge all the impact. Without completely dealing with these wounds, a stronghold or entry point for dark spirits remains.

Remember, when we are in a place of disobedience, we allow the demons a place of vulnerability in our soul to attack. A typical complication which often surfaces during inner healing work is the presence of unforgiveness in one's life. This is so common that we generally will begin working through forgiveness prior to any other work with a client. It is also rare to have a client that does not have any issue of forgiveness to address.

> The LORD is merciful and gracious, slow to anger and abounding in steadfast love. He will not always chide, nor will He keep His anger forever. He does not deal with us according to our sins, nor repay us according to our iniquities. For as high as the heavens are above the earth, so great is His steadfast love toward those who fear him; as far as

the east is from the west, so far does he remove our transgressions from us. (Psalm 103:8-12)

There is a popular notion that forgiveness involves forgetting. Nonsense, God created our brains to store information so we could learn from our experiences. Forgiveness does not require forgetting OR reconciliation. We do come to a point of "forgetting" to count an offense against someone; a point that a particular hurt isn't used as fuel for an argument or seeking revenge.

Forgiveness is a process and decision to let go of the right to remain hurt or offended. Remember, Jesus answered to forgive seventy times seven when asked how many times we should forgive another (Matthew 18:22). There are situations that make forgiving seem impossible. In these instances, we must give the emotional injury and offense to God and ask Him to remove the burden. You may find a relative ease of offering forgiveness to the other party once God has healed the hurt within you.

Having to repeatedly address a disgruntled spirit and choosing to forgive, *again*, does not mean that you didn't really forgive the first time. Rather, it often simply means that the wound was very deep.

EVENT

EMOTIONAL REACTION
- assign blame
- anger
- grief

JOURNAL AND SHARE THE STORY (REPEATEDLY)
- justification of viewpoint
- processing event
- accepting appropriate responsibility

CHOOSE ACTION
- hyper-focus on event
- fantasize about retribution
- choose to ignore the event
- decide to forgive

In any situation requiring forgiveness, there is an initiating event in which the offense or injury occurs due to one's perspective of the catalyst. Through personal biases, one experiences emotional reactions, such as assigning blame, feeling angry, or grieving something we have lost, e.g., trust. As one moves through the emotional reaction(s), the natural focus is to begin processing what happened. Methods of processing include journaling and/or sharing the story with others. It is possible to continue cycling through this portion of processing for a while before choosing an action, because attempts to justify a personal viewpoint or accepting appropriate individual responsibility is difficult. Sometimes, an action is chosen by default rather than deliberation. In such cases, one may feel "stuck" and hyper-focus on the event or fantasize about retribution. It is also possible that one employs denial or ignores the event thinking that avoiding conflict of any kind is the better choice. Avoidance never addresses the root issue. The action that gives the greatest freedom is the decision to forgive.

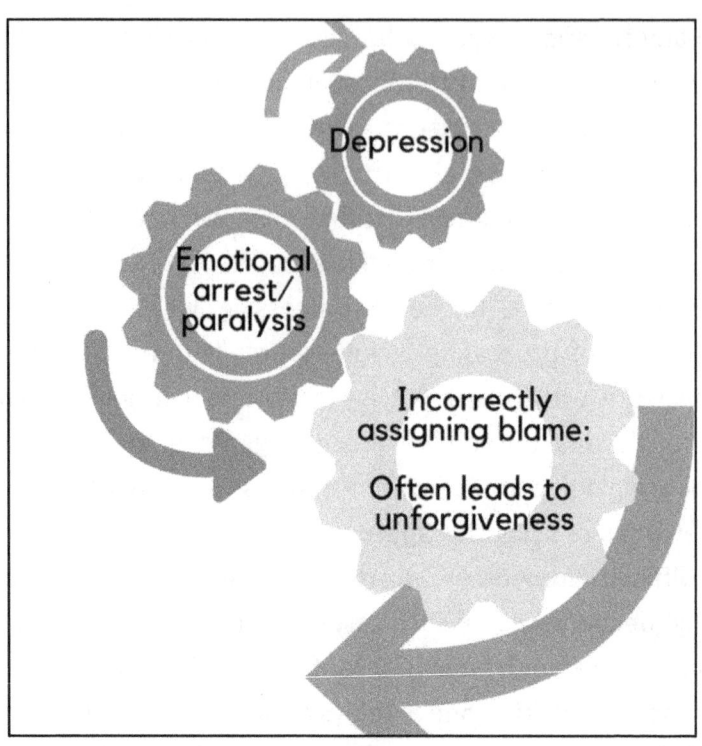

Continuing to operate in unforgiveness is often a function of multiple interlocking reactions. If blame is incorrectly assigned, it is possible to experience both emotional paralysis and depression. Each of these functions can facilitate and exacerbate the other(s), keeping one in bondage due to unforgiveness.

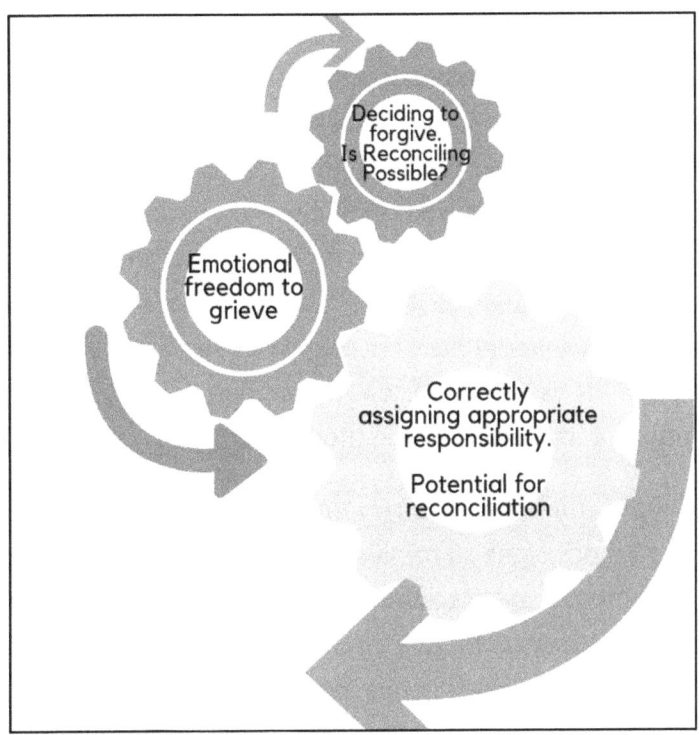

Correctly assigning responsibility provides greater potential for reconciliation after forgiveness has been granted. The interplay in this process includes assessing if reconciliation is a healthy and mutually beneficial aspect of moving forward. Within the context of forgiving and potentially reconciling, there is a freedom to grieve what was, or even what was hoped for, that can no longer be simply because of the breach that occurred. This is not necessarily a systematic or linear process, so please recognize that moving in and out of the various areas does not necessarily mean you are not moving toward reconciliation.

Forgiveness is a deliberate decision. One chooses to forgive, it doesn't simply occur because you stayed within a certain acceptable range of emotion in reaction to the offense. If you do not choose to surrender the right to be hurt, then by default, you retain the right to be hurt and can use that at any point in the future against the offender. When you choose to retain the right to remain hurt, offended, or wounded, you choose to remain a victim by default. It is very difficult to be both a victim and a conqueror at the same time (Romans 8:37).

We have found that forgiveness is often a process of repeated decisions to forgive. The deeper the wound, the more times we need to choose to release the offender. It's a nice concept to forgive once and then it is done. This works with the minor issues, but rarely with the big hurts. Know that each time you choose to forgive, you are weakening the enemy.

Since reconciliation is not commanded, we can forgive without having to continue to be harmed. For those of you wondering about the instruction in Matthew 5:23-24 to "leave your offering at the altar and go and be reconciled," let's look a little closer at the relationship being described, as well as the word being translated as "reconciled." In this instance, you are the one who has offended another. In such circumstances, you are commanded to go to the other and attempt repair of the relationship by accepting responsibility and asking for their forgiveness. You are instructed to work toward change. The change may be an agreement to discontinue a relationship amicably rather than continuing the separation with lingering angst.

The word used in these two verses is *diallasso,* and it is only used once in Scripture. It is a combination of the words *dia* and *allasso.* It communicates an expectation that you are to seek to repair a relationship (initiate a move toward change) even if you are innocent of all accusations. The Amplified Bible translates *diallasso* as "peace." Your role in the relationship is significant in the application of the term interpreted as "reconciled." There is a qualifier; inasmuch as it depends on you (Hebrews 12:14). The other person could make proceeding in peace impossible because of their behavior and attitudes. It still rests on you to conduct yourself in a manner appropriate for Christ's ambassador.

Reconciliation is important and may even be a part of the process of forgiveness. We need to seek the Holy Spirit's direction to know what He desires. The decision to reconcile is separate from the decision to forgive.

There are situations when one extends forgiveness but going back into the relationship with the offender could be detrimental. We exercise forgiveness and choose to live in peace rather than reengaging an ongoing relationship. Other times, we need to forgive people that are deceased or from the past which precludes being able to go further than extending forgiveness.

As Christians, forgiving those around us gives us an opportunity to attest to what God has done for us. It is important that we not wear our forgiveness as a badge of honor, and we must be careful not to dishonor those we've forgiven by telling the story. We can share the process that God took us through and how He has provided freedom through the act of forgiveness. This may help another to take the steps they need to be free.

Remember, unforgiveness is sinful on your part and gives the enemy a legal right to harass you. "A legal right is sinful behavior that has not been repented of . . . a legal right is how the devil gets in. The stronghold is how he stays in. A stronghold is a place of emotional investment [or obsession] in your life. Satan intensifies that emotion until it's over the edge and controls your actions." (Larson, B. *Demon Proofing Prayers*, Pg. 32)

If you have unforgiveness, you need to deal with that before moving forward in spiritual battle. Because each situation is unique to the individual, there may be other sin issues that need to be confessed. No sin merits greater or lesser penalty under God's law; all sin is equal. The reason unforgiveness receives so much attention in our material is that it by far seems to be the one area that can be a lynchpin in delaying progress.

Unforgiveness is a way Satan gains an entry point that may become a stronghold in your life. It becomes a place of vulnerability. The problem is the devil isn't content with stopping there. He wants as much of your physical, mental, emotional, and spiritual being as he can control. Remember, he's power-hungry. Your unforgiveness feeds his quest for more and more control and power, AND it keeps you trapped by the gates of hell.

Unforgiveness can come in the form of constantly blaming. Let's take a closer look at assigning blame.

> Blaming only causes us to deny our responsibility and to point our fingers at someone or something other than ourselves. In essence, this describes a victim mentality. But the painful truth is that *we* are the real problem. We have a heart that is evil and often chooses sin over righteousness! (Jackson, J. *Needless Casualties of War*, pg. 39).

Blame is a never-ending cycle of hurt, accusation, and finger pointing. Unless we are willing to take the responsibility for our part of the situation and forgive the other participants for theirs, we will be unable to break the cycle.

For some, you will need to forgive yourself. While the Bible does not command or prohibit this, Satan, as an accuser of the saints, often uses our failure to forgive ourselves to render us less effective. If God has forgiven you in response to your repentance, it becomes sinful for you to dwell on that act and not forgive yourself. It becomes sinful the very moment you decide you know better than God. In that moment, you are choosing not only to accuse and condemn yourself, but you become an idolater by raising yourself to higher authority than our Heavenly Father. What's that? Oh, yes, that mimics exactly what Satan did when He was cast out of Heaven. It's dangerous and treacherous ground. Don't live there.

****

There are times when forgiving is extremely difficult. Dallas shares a fraction of her journey to forgive through this allegorical story (the names and some details have been changed to protect the innocent and guilty).

As you read the following story, if someone comes to mind from your past hurts that you need to forgive, write it down in the margin and transfer it later to the end of the chapter.

When I was 27, my husband and I were expecting our fourth child. We moved to Colorado Springs just after Mark graduated and started settling our family. That meant finding a job, we moved in complete faith without any means of supporting ourselves, housing, and all the other social support that comes with a major move. We were excited about this next child and hoped for a smooth pregnancy and delivery. Unfortunately, early in the second trimester we miscarried. That was a very painful time for us. We sought out a church family that could minister to us, and eventually, we started to find places in the church that we could fill and minister to others. After a time, we discovered that we were ready to try to have another child, and set about making the preparations: adequate space, furnishings, and decorations. The dreams and plans started to take shape.

My husband turned 32 that year. The pregnancy went as most do; the norm with morning sickness and fatigue. We started looking for additional help and continued more fervently when we realized that we would be delivering a special needs child. Along the way, we were disappointed multiple times when promises and expectations were left unfulfilled. There were several significant blows. People avoided us. People told us we must have done something wrong. People advised us to abort. Someone actually told my husband we appeared to be unfit parents and said if things didn't change within a certain amount of time, our child would be taken away from us.

There were still neighbors that were pregnant and having baby showers. I just couldn't go. It was hard enough to receive and read an invitation.

My mother-in-law decided to move closer to help. She didn't have any more commitments that would prevent her relocation, and she wanted to be closer to her grandchildren. She was an immense help; one of those ladies who will step up to a challenge and handle it with grace. She would stay and help for three years.

As any parent of more than one child knows, when one family member is struggling, it doesn't preclude others from facing various difficulties. When you have several people in the same household, things can become a very stressful juggling act. There are physical ailments, emotional distress, relationship issues, academic difficulties, professional demands, and other numerous internal and external pressures that each member must face.

If one is blessed enough to be a parent, you are faced with the task of helping your children navigate these psychologically, sociologically, and spiritually choppy waters. Our family is no different. Even during struggling to find the best support and treatments for our fifth child, our first remained angry that we moved away from her friends and that she was not an only child. Our twins faced more of the normal pressures of growing up, but those have presented their own unique challenges, primarily in the academic arena where the "professionals" continually try to convince us that as parents we are ignorant of our children's academic abilities, personalities, and learning styles. Try dealing with that after having already been trampled by the people professing to be those with whom faith and trust would always be available.

The health of our fifth child continued to be an uphill battle. The doctors suggested several different individuals to provide home care. We would meet with them, hire them, and then shortly thereafter, they would leave and we would be on our own again. There were too many to name.

Then, we met Newman Nathair. We had some prior knowledge of Newman's work from others in town. People were in one of two schools of thought regarding Newman. Either they loved him or they hated him. We had dinner together to talk through how things would change if Newman were hired. He seemed energetic and capable. There were concerns, though. The more we got to know Mr. Nathair, the more we felt as if it were vitally important to him that he become our daughter, Naomi's sole support. To the best of our ability, we remained connected and involved in all our normal family activities. Then one day, I received an email from Newman. He had arranged for a cook to come. I loved cooking and followed a carefully planned diet for our daughter, so it hurt to be replaced under the guise of trying to be helpful. Newman didn't seem to respect that my, nor my husband's, decisions were always in the best interest of our child. He continually told her what she *wanted* to hear or "*aided*" her in making decisions like what to wear by subliminally cloaking questions as statements to which she readily agreed without reserve.

We felt an immense amount of burden and responsibility, but sensed that our children saw our instructions as unnecessary. We had been the seemingly isolated and solely active watchdogs for all our children for so long that we had no energy left to fight Newman's manipulation. Then Newman suggested that it would be easier to care for our child if we were not in the immediate environment, and we were separated from her forever.

Secretly, we wished that our daughter, Naomi, would run away and come back to us, but we could never suggest such behavior. We hoped that even at her early age, she would see that what was happening was wrong. She did manage to find us once, but Newman followed her, so she couldn't completely get away.

Occasionally, we would receive reports from others that had seen our daughter, because they had been out of town on trips and what not. While it hurt that they got to see our daughter, it devastated me further when they started reporting that she looked great but wasn't acting like herself. "You need to let them know they are dropping the ball and need to get things back together." Oh, if only that were possible.

Then we saw in the newspaper that the facility where she resided was being bought out by another company. My husband had prior knowledge of the individual in charge; and therefore, we were immediately alarmed. A few weeks later, we received word that our child had passed away. Grief stricken, I went about preparing for the funeral.

I knew this was coming, so I had already done some of the preliminary research on florists and gravestone markers. I ordered the headstone to read "Naomi – We loved you greatly and gave you everything we had. We wish it had been enough." There was an error however, so when it was unveiled at the gravesite, it instead read "Marah." We did not have the headstone redone. Bitter seemed to communicate a substantial portion of our recent experience. I remain disappointed to this day, wishing to honor the memory of the daughter I knew and feeling so betrayed by what was placed at her grave.

My grief was deeply complicated by the fact that there was no true acknowledgement that Naomi had died. Occasionally, someone would offer a "How are you doing?" or "Let's grab lunch." However, mostly, we were ignored and even shunned.

I sobbed for days; I was angry at God. Even years after she was taken from us, I still sobbed, and was still VERY angry with God. I was faithful to invest my time and energy with nothing in return except heartache and a broken family. My marriage suffered, my relationships with my other children were not as strong as they could have been, and in my darkest moments, I contemplated whether I wanted to remain on earth knowing that the pain might never go away.

****

Not only have we had to forgive each of those that offended us in the reality represented by the allegorical situation in the above story, but we have also had to seek forgiveness from those that we unintentionally hurt in the process. It took a long time, but Dallas finally came to the place where she completely let go of the attitude that she was entitled to remain offended and hurt (Translation: able to forgive). We came to the realization that, had God not allowed all the circumstances that created such hurt and heartache, we would be less able to relate to others, and we would not have grown in our spiritual walk thereby growing closer to Him in His fullness.

We find that individuals frequently must deal with the far removed past, as well as the not so distant past, when they are actively forgiving. Maybe that applies to you. Take a moment to look at your life's timeline. Where are there unhealed hurts? How old are you in each of those events? None of these take our Heavenly Father by surprise. He didn't cause them, but He didn't prevent them either. If you are angry at God for not intervening, perhaps you need to start by forgiving God. God is perfect and doesn't need our forgiveness, but for us to be restored and reconciled to Him, we forgive Him to fully relinquish the right to see Him as being unjust.

INNER HEALING EXERCISE

Think about past experiences that have distressing emotions still attached to them or those memories that had an intense reaction at the time it occurred. Did someone scare you as a child; did your young child scare or embarrass you as a parent; did a friend say something behind your back? Even these seemingly small issues that you may have locked away can have an impact in the spiritual realm.

* Who do you need to ask to forgive you?

* Who do you need to forgive?

* What hurt do you need to ask God to heal to make forgiveness toward the offender easier and complete?

* What do you need God to do for you to be able to let go of your "right" to hold on to unforgiveness?

You can ask God for a heart that can forgive just like you can ask for more faith. Ask Jesus to stand with you as you see those that have hurt you line up. As each one passes, say, "None of us deserve forgiveness, but I choose to forgive. I forgive you for _____."

DOORS, LEGAL RIGHTS, AND STRONGHOLDS

The premise of the existence of a court system, and therefore legal rights within the spiritual realm, is derived by multiple Scripture references that use legal terms and refer to God as our Judge. Sections of Job revolve around an arbiter, a summary defense, and a final appeal. Other legal terms found in Scripture are names such as Advocate (Jesus Christ), accuser (Satan), and in Zechariah 3:6, it specifically says "my courts" (1 Samuel 24:15, Job 1:6-12, 2:1-6; Psalm 9:8, 50:6, 75:7, 82:1; Isaiah 33:22, Daniel 7:9-10, James 4:11-12, 1 Peter 4:5, Revelation 20:11-15).

Satan and his minions gain access to our lives through doors that have been opened. They get to stay if they perceive a legal right to that access. Some legal rights lead to strongholds that the enemy builds. In this chapter, we are going to discuss some of the many doors that the evil one uses and how to break legal rights. We are also going to examine strongholds—both of the enemy and of God.

When we enter a building, we go through a door. And then once inside the building, we may go into different rooms through various doorways. The spirit realm is the same. Spirits, both good and evil, enter through doors in our lives. We need to be sure that we lock and bar the doors that allow the evil spirits to enter and to open the doors for the Holy Spirit to come in and dwell in us.

DOORS

Spiritual doors typically fall into the following categories:
1. Things we have done
2. Things others have done to us
3. Generational

We spent time talking about the importance of forgiveness. Since unforgiveness is a sin (Matthew 6:14-15, Mark 11:25-26), it allows unholy access to our lives—a door. Other sins also open doors for the evil one to enter. Think about the effects of unrighteous anger.

There is a difference between a holy or righteous anger and a soulish or unrighteous anger. It is not the anger itself that is a sin. Remember, Jesus displayed a holy anger when the merchants were turning God's house into a den of robbers. The motivation and the action taken when we feel the anger is what determines the type. "Be angry and do not sin" (Psalms 4:4, Ephesians 4:26a).

When we choose to sin and choose to remain in that sin, we are opening doors. The longer we leave the door open, the greater number of evil spirits we allow entrance, and the stronger they become (Ephesians 4:27, Colossians 3:5-9, James 1:14-15, 19-21).

Have you ever played with a Ouija board? What about experimentation with the "game" Dungeons and Dragons? Have you ever consulted a horoscope, psychic, used Tarot Cards or Angel Cards? Did you ever engage in attempts at levitation or achieving self-hypnosis or permit yourself to be hypnotized? You may have thought that these were just games or a fun activity. They are far more than a game. These are all doors that allow the evil one access to our lives (Leviticus 20:6, Deuteronomy 18:9-12).

We are personally aware of at least one occasion in which a fortune teller was invited to a high school event as a club fundraiser. Prayers covered this event and the individual wound up not attending at all. God spared the community from that demonic exposure and impact.

Often, doors are opened by others. Child abuse opens doors that the evil one uses to hold people hostage for many years. The child did not open the door and didn't have any ability to stop the abuse, but a door was created for the evil one to access them. Most abuse, physical, sexual, mental, verbal, spiritual, or financial, will result in an *opportunity* for the spirits of darkness to enter and set up a stronghold in a person's life. These are vulnerabilities into a person's soul, not a definite infiltration by the enemy. When working toward healing, it is common to have to address these open doors and determine what spirits, if any, have entered. It may be necessary to release a person's will to enable them to make decisions that permit Christ to have Lordship.

One of our positions is that you do not have to know the specific names of dark spirits to command them to leave. The lying spirit can weary you by suggesting a plethora of incorrect names to be commanded away. You can command them by function or behavior that is manifesting; however, if there is a list of spirits which appear to be working in tandem, the specific grouping may help inform one that there is a particular stronghold present which must be addressed.

We have found that participation in occult activities often results in legal rights and strongholds that pass to future generations. For example, membership, or a family member's membership, in a Masonic lodge is a common generational door that we have had to deal with and cut off. (There are many resources for further research on

Freemasonry and how its teachings compare to the Holy Bible; however, that is beyond the scope of this book).

We have also found that generational curses give the evil one access and often legal rights to a person. Scripture says, ". . . visiting the iniquity of the fathers on the children and the children's children, to the third and the fourth generation." (Exodus 20:5; Exodus 34:7; Numbers 14:18 and Deuteronomy 5:9). We have the power to cut off these generational curses under the new covenant of Christ (Jeremiah 31:29-30; Galatians 3:23-26). It is unclear how God determines which curses are permitted to pass to others and which are kept from becoming generational in nature. Because of the existence of Scriptures that indicate both positions, we acknowledge this as a *possible* breach in one's soul rather than an absolute.

God does not tolerate, excuse, or ignore sin. Whether the door is accessed through the legal right of an assignment or agreement, we must address it, and with the help of the Holy Spirit, clean house and secure the door(s). You can pray that Christ will secure the door by covering it with His Blood. Please remember, that God respects our free will. You can give up ground taken by returning to old habits, thought patterns, and a sinful lifestyle. Culturally, there is a door of complacency (e.g., tolerance of socially accepted behaviors that go against God's commands). Complacency is an agreement to not challenge these sinful behaviors.

Remember, when you challenge a behavior, show love to the person and ask God to provide conviction and correction, because He knows best how to both discipline and woo those whom He loves. The Holy Spirit is the One responsible for conviction and will instruct you as to whether you should address the action with another directly or not. Use spiritual discernment, not fleshly judgement.

Now, let's consider doors that allow the Holy Spirit to come into and fill our lives. Healthy spiritual habits are good doors. These include prayer, Scripture reading, fasting, worship, biblical community, serving others, and giving. When we focus our lives and devote our time and resources to the things of God, we open the door to become filled with even more of Him.

We could expound on each of these types of doors, but for now, let's limit ourselves to considering Scripture reading. When we use our time reading and studying God's words, we are allowing Him to replace false beliefs with the Truth. We are told in Timothy:

> All Scripture is given by inspiration of God, and is profitable for doctrine, for reproof, for correction, for instruction in righteousness, that the man of God

may be complete, thoroughly equipped for every good work (2 Timothy 3:16 NKJV).

LEGAL RIGHTS

In the spirit world, there are rules and laws much like we have here in America. In business, we use contracts on a regular basis. Contracts identify the parties involved, what each party is expected to do, and what each must receive. A contract is legally binding upon all the parties that sign it. Contracts establish legal rights.

We also create contracts in the spirit realms through agreements, curses, vows, and judgements. Far too often, we don't even realize that we have created such a contract. Think about a time that you made a rash statement such as, "I swear, I will/I will never _____" or "You are so stupid" or "You are just like your mother/father." In these statements, we may have set up a vow, judgment, or a curse in our own life or the life of another.

We dealt with a young lady who had made a vow that she would receive all the negatives, so her sister could receive the positives. Her mother received a word of knowledge and short vision regarding this vow; otherwise, it may have remained hidden and continued to impact her life negatively. The mother reports a vision of seeing her oldest child in the hospital room visiting the newborn and saying, "You (devil) can do whatever you want to me if you'll leave her alone." When you look at the vow/agreement, it appears to be quite loving and generous to sacrifice your own happiness for the sake of the other; however, if you looked at the family as a whole, the vow actually made relational dynamics quite difficult at times as it seemed no one could appease this young lady. We had her confess the agreement, ask for forgiveness, and then cancel it out with the Blood of Christ. The reported transformation of this individual from what she had been to what she has become is remarkable.

Words are powerful. In James 3, we are told that the tongue is a small part of the body but is extremely powerful. James 3:3-6 says:

> If we put bits into the mouths of horses so that they obey us, we guide their whole bodies as well. Look at the ships also: though they are so large and are driven by strong winds, they are guided by a very small rudder wherever the will of the pilot directs. So also the tongue is a small member, yet it boast of great things.
>
> How great a forest is set ablaze by such a small fire! And the tongue is a fire, a world of unrighteousness. The tongue is set among our members, staining the

whole body, setting on fire the entire course of life, and set on fire by hell.

Even though some legally binding contracts are required to be in writing, in the spirit realm legal rights can be established through spoken words or even thoughts. In the Sermon on the Mount Jesus says, "I say to you that everyone who looks at a woman with lustful intent has already committed adultery with her in his heart" (Matthew 6). It is extremely important that we take captive every thought to obey Christ.

> For though we walk in the flesh, we are not waging war according to the flesh. For the weapons of our warfare are not of the flesh but have divine power to destroy strongholds. We destroy arguments and every lofty opinion raised against the knowledge of God, and take every thought captive to obey Christ, being ready to punish every disobedience, when your obedience is complete. (2 Corinthians 10:3-6)

The good news is that we can also break these legal rights of the evil one with a repentant attitude and the confession of our words. Please don't misunderstand. There is no power in the arrangement of the words. It is not the same as those involved in evil hexes, curses, and spells where the words are formulaic and given in a specific order. The intent of the heart is what God considers. When we repent of our sin and renounce the right of the evil one, we can be set free. The price of the contract still must be paid, though. Fortunately, we have a Savior, Jesus Christ, Who has paid for our sins and who will void the contracts that we have made.

When we commit our life to Christ, we are establishing a legal right that He has over us. Think about a soldier that enlists in the Army. The enlistment is a contract in which the soldier agrees to be subject to the rules and follow the commands of the Army. I've often wondered why someone would be willing to subject themselves to such strict standards. A soldier is not his own but is completely under the control of his commander. If the commander says in the middle of the night that the soldier is to get up and hike ten miles, that is what the soldier does. A soldier agrees to behave in a certain manner. In return, the soldier can expect a paycheck, heath care, and job security.

As members of the army of Christ, we are held to strict standards. We are not our own, for we were bought with a price. "Or do you not know that your body is a temple of the Holy Spirit within you, whom you have from God? You are not your own, for you were bought with a price. So glorify God in your body" (1 Corinthians 6:19-20). When our Commander wakes us up in the middle of the night, we are to get up and do what He says. It is common for us to be awakened and spend an hour or more in prayer. When we are faithful in our calling, then God is faithful in His provisions and answers.

STRONGHOLDS

Strongholds are well established, protected areas in our lives. The Webster definition of stronghold is "an area where most people have the same beliefs, values, etc.; an area dominated by a particular group; a protected place where the members of a military group stay and can defend themselves against attacks." While doors could be compared to a beachhead, a stronghold is like a castle on the bluff above the beach that has been fortified.

Strongholds are not established overnight. They take time and effort to develop and are often reinforced in our thought life, as well as our behaviors.

We discussed earlier that sin provides an open door for the evil one to enter our lives. When we continue in that sin, the evil spirit gets comfortable, sets up house and may even invite others to join in our lives. The longer we remain in sin, the stronger the presence becomes, and eventually there will be a stronghold in our life.

Have you or someone you know struggled with an addiction? Think of someone who smokes. That first cigarette opened the door. The continuation of smoking established the physical desire and need for even more. Most likely a smoker isn't going to be able to tell you the day that they became addicted and could no longer just stop. It happened over time with the repeated partaking of the addicting item. Once addicted, it is very difficult to stop. It takes a very concerted effort to overcome the effects of withdrawal. In some rare situations, I've heard of people that quit cold turkey, but most take time.

In spiritual strongholds, we have found that the Holy Spirit is powerful enough to free the captives immediately, but sometimes it takes considerable time and effort to break the chains of bondage. We will discuss in a later section the process of deliverance.

Just as with doors and legal rights, strongholds can be for evil, or they may be holy. Francis Frangipane says that humility is a stronghold of the Godly.

> Satan fears virtue. He is terrified of humility; he hates it. He sees a humble person and it sends chills down his back. His hair stands up when Christians kneel down, for humility is the surrender of the soul to God. The devil trembles before the meek because in the very areas where he once had access, there stands the Lord, and Satan is terrified of Jesus

Christ. (Frangipane, F. *The Three Battlegrounds,* Pg. 21)

The strength of humility is that it builds a spiritual defense around your soul, prohibiting strife, competition and many of life's irritations from stealing your peace. (Frangipane, F. *The Three Battlegrounds,* Pg. 25)

We need to be diligent to replace the unholy with the holy (Ephesians 4:17-24, 1 Peter 1:14-16). It is important that we examine our lives, with the help of the Holy Spirit, removing anything that may give the enemy an entrance or place of dwelling. Equally vital is to fill our lives with the things of God and operate in the fruit of the Spirit (Galatians 5:22-23).

CHAPTER QUESTIONS

* What unholy doors have you opened?

* What holy doors have you opened?

* What doors, legal rights, or strongholds need to be addressed in your life?

BELIEVERS' AUTHORITY IN CHRIST

Authority, or the Greek word *exousia*, is defined as having the power or right to give orders, make decisions, and enforce obedience. Authority can be granted to someone only by another who is higher in rank. We discussed in the prior chapter about how we may grant legal rights similar to a contract in the business world. You must have the proper authority when signing a contract. Generally, you should have a position sufficient to give you that authority.

For example, if you walked into a bank and said that you wanted to borrow money in the name of a corporation, the banker will require you to be authorized by the legal documents of the corporation to borrow the funds. You may act on behalf of the corporation only to the extent that you are authorized to do so.

There is no higher authority than God, and He grants authority to men. Romans 13:1 says, "Let every person be subject to the governing authorities. For there is no authority except from God, and those that exist have been instituted by God." We often feel a need to rebel against the authority figures in our world if we do not agree with their positions or their actions. This verse tells us that even the evil authority figures have been put in place by God.

What grants us the authority to fight in the spiritual realm? The blood of Christ and the salvation His blood provides grant us the authority. The authority is not conveyed outside of the power and Holy Name of Jesus Christ. There is no other way we are authorized as Christian soldiers.

When Jesus sent out his disciples, He gave them authority. Mark 6:7 says, "And He called the twelve and began to send them out two by two, and gave them authority over the unclean spirits." When we go about the work of God's kingdom, it is in Christ's authority that we are going; any other authority will be insufficient. In Luke 10:19 Jesus says, "Behold, I have given you authority to tread on serpents and scorpions, and over all the power of the enemy, and nothing shall hurt you."

In Matthew 28:18-20, "And Jesus came and said to them, 'All authority in heaven and on earth has been given to me. Go therefore and make disciples of all the nations, baptizing them in the name of the Father and of the Son and of the Holy Spirit, teaching them to observe all that I have commanded you. And behold, I am with you always, to the end of the age.'"

Jesus began by establishing that He has been given all authority in heaven and on earth. Jesus came to earth in the authority of the Father. "The words that I say to you I do not speak on my own authority, but the Father who dwells in me does His works" (John 14:10). "As I myself have received authority from my Father" (Revelation 2:27).

The rest of the passage in Revelation says, "The one who conquers and who keeps my works until the end, to him I will give authority over the nations, and he will rule them with a rod of iron, as when earthen pots are broken in pieces, even as I myself have received authority from my Father" (Revelation 2:26-27). Notice that the authority is granted to the one who keeps Christ's works until the end. We must be in constant obedience to the will of God to operate in His authority. John Paul Jackson says, "To be given spiritual authority requires that we humbly submit to God's authority" (Jackson, J. *Needless Casualties of War,* Pg. 68).

We also see in John 14:21, "Whoever has my commands and keeps them, he it is who loves Me. And he who loves Me will be loved by my Father, and I will love him and manifest Myself to him." We cannot put enough emphasis on the importance of our walking in obedience before we attempt to go into battle. If we are not obedient, then we will have a place of vulnerability to the evil one. Effectively, there will be a breach in the battle line.

After having some success in deliverance ministry, it is easy to start to think that we have it figured out and can handle it on our own. In other words, we can become prideful. We will never be able to successfully wage war on the enemy without the authority and power bestowed on us through Christ. Be careful to not allow pride to work its way into your heart.

When we battle in the spirit realm, it is not in our own authority but in Christ's authority. Also, we do not battle with our own power and strength. We must battle with the direction of the Holy Spirit and the power of the Blood of Christ.

> And I heard a loud voice in heaven, saying, "Now the salvation and the power and the kingdom of our God and the authority of his Christ have come, for the accuser of our brothers has been thrown down, who accuses them day and night before our God. And they have conquered him by the blood of the Lamb and by the word of their testimony, for they loved not their lives even unto death.
> (Revelation 12:10-11)

Let's look at some of the characteristics and work of Christ's blood.

1. Christ's blood provides forgiveness of sin.
    - "Without the shedding of blood there is no forgiveness of sin." Hebrews 9:22
    - "The blood of Jesus His Son cleanses us from all sin." 1 John 1:7
    - "How much more will the blood of Christ, who through the eternal Spirit offered Himself without blemish to God, purify our conscience from dead works to serve the living God." Hebrews 9:14

2. We are bought by the blood of Christ.
    - "And there is salvation in no one else, for there is no other name under heaven given among men by which we must be saved." Acts 4:12
    - "Knowing that you were ransomed from the futile ways inherited from your forefathers, not with perishable things such as silver or gold, but with the precious blood of Christ, like that of a lamb without blemish or spot." 1 Peter 1:18-19

3. Christ's blood provides protection.
    - "Therefore, brothers, since we have confidence to enter the holy places by the blood of Jesus," Hebrews 10:19

- "The blood shall be a sign for you, on the houses where you are. And when I see the blood, I will pass over you, and no plague will befall you to destroy you, when I strike the land of Egypt." Exodus 12:13

Battling in the spirit realm isn't just the job of spiritual leaders. Mattheus Van Der Steen says, "We all [that is Believers in Christ] have a responsibility . . . . We all have authority; we all can bring in the Kingdom of God here on this Earth." (*Furious Love*, Deluxe Edition. Darren Wilson. Wanderlust Productions, 2010. DVD).

We will do what Christ did and more. "Truly, truly, I say to you, whoever believes in Me will also do the works that I do; and greater works than these will he do, because I am going to the Father" (John 14:12).

While there is some debate as to what Christ meant when He made this statement, we believe that it means we have the ability to perform all of the miracles that Christ performed and even more as the Father directs and the Holy Spirit empowers. The important thing is that we operate in complete submission to the Father, as Christ did, and work in the power granted us through the Blood of Christ. Our lives are a journey with the Lord, doing as He directs; loving as He loves; and going where He goes.

Mark 16:17-18, And these signs will accompany those who believe: in my name they will cast out demons; they will speak in new tongues; they will pick up serpents with their hands; and if they drink any deadly poison, it will not hurt them; they will lay their hands on the sick, and they will recover.

How do we know what works we are to be doing? The only way to know is through the direction of the Holy Spirit. In Acts 1:8, Jesus told the disciples to wait until they had the Holy Spirit, and then they were to go out into the entire world proclaiming the gospel. God is three in one – the Father, the Son and the Holy Spirit. Each is 100% God and each is also unique in His function. The Holy Spirit is called a helper or counselor (John 14:16). John 14:26 says, "But the Helper, the Holy Spirit, whom the Father will send in My name, He will teach you all things and bring to your remembrance all that I have said to you."

What a good promise to rely on; the Holy Spirit will remind you. Dallas has found this to be true on more than one occasion. There was one experience early on when Mark had taken the lead in ministry, and then sensed he needed to pass off that portion of commanding to Dallas as the Holy Spirit was giving her words of knowledge to deal with the current circumstances and unclean spiritual attachments. Suddenly, slightly panicked, she stopped and said, "I don't remember what to do." Mark was dumbfounded, because much of what needed to be done, Dallas had learned to do before he did. He broke the spirits off that were causing the memory impairment and confusion and asked the Holy Spirit to remind Dallas what needed to be done.

We must wait upon the direction of the Holy Spirit to know where to go, what to say, and what to do. This may sound easy, but far too often, we run ahead or lag behind the Spirit's direction. We must learn how to hear the voice of our Master, and then, we must respond. As Pastor Che Ahn said, "We must put expression to the impression." (*Holy Ghost*, Deluxe Edition. Darren Wilson. Wanderlust Productions, 2014. DVD Disc 3). In other words, when the Spirit provides direction, we must notice and act accordingly.

Jesus said, ". . . for they know His voice. A stranger they will not follow, but they will flee from him, for they do not know the voice of strangers." (John 10:4-5) We must be in communication with the Spirit to learn what His voice sounds like, so that we will recognize it. When we know His voice, we will also know when the evil one attempts to bring counterfeit messages.

Two of the gifts of the Spirit that are of great benefit in spiritual warfare are discernment and words of knowledge. Like many of the gifts, we need to be in communion with the Holy Spirit to operate effectively in them. Discernment will often allow us to know when to move forward, to stop, or to shift directions. It is also helpful to be able to discern when we are dealing with lies or distractions of the enemy.

Words of knowledge provide information about the enemy such as what spirits are present. Since the evil spirits are natural liars it is best not to depend on them for information such as their identity or how many are present. The Holy Spirit is able to provide us the information that is needed and often does so through words of knowledge.

As we grow in our closeness to Christ and humbly submit to Him, we will be able to know the clear directions. When we hear clearly, we can proceed in battle in the authority and power of Christ. That is when we will be victorious.

CHAPTER QUESTIONS

* What must we do to operate in God's authority?
* What are some characteristics of the blood of Christ?
* How do we know what works we are to be doing?

PROTECTION AFTER THE BATTLE

There are some extra protective precautions that should be taken after deliverance work or after any advancement of God's Kingdom against the gates of hell. These include sealing off previously tainted and vulnerable areas, filling the opened spaces with the fruit of the Holy Spirit, praying against the anger of Satan and its effects, praying against retribution or retaliation on the part of the enemy, as well as against any re-establishment of assignments that have been broken.

"Sealing off" is the process of asking God to cover that place with the blood of Christ and post a guard to help defend against the enemy, so that when the unclean spirits return hoping to find a home again, they will be unsuccessful.

> When the unclean spirit has gone out of a person, it passes through waterless places seeking rest, and

finding none it says, 'I will return to my house from which I came.' And when it comes, it finds the house swept and put in order. Then it goes and brings seven other spirits more evil than itself, and they enter and dwell there. And the last state of that person is worse than the first. (Luke 11:24-26)

Ask that the Holy Spirit will come fill the void left from the removal of the evil spirit. We often request the Holy Spirit to put in the opposite of what was removed. For example, if doubt was cast out, ask for faith to replace it. A great source for good things to fill a space is the fruit of the Spirit as listed in Galatians 5:22-23. "But the fruit of the Spirit is love, joy, peace, patience, kindness, goodness, faithfulness, gentleness, self-control; against such things there is on law."

Personal decisions may weaken any seal that has been placed by God, as He respects our right to choose. If the persons who experienced deliverance are unwilling to submit to the authority of Christ in their lives, they will be vulnerable to future attack and may result with a worse state than before the deliverance. This is the reason we choose to inquire about salvation prior to beginning deliverance work. There are times when leaving individuals in their current state is more merciful than creating an environment for even more spiritual oppression. While we want freedom and release for the individual, we follow God's example of allowing each one to choose who will be in control of their life.

Earlier, there was a mention of praying to release the person's will. Remember a person's will is housed in their soul not their spirit. Without being able to take thoughts captive to come into agreement with God's Truth, a bound will can prevent one from being able to exercise a decision to follow Christ. God has given man a free will, yet the enemy wants to make us believe that we do not have freedom to decide. In such an instance, the enemy has attempted to prevent a person's salvation.

It is important to follow deliverance work with a discipleship program. While the initial freedom may seem complete, the individual probably has patterns of behavior or false beliefs that need to be corrected to maintain that freedom.

Praying against the anger of Satan, in any form it may take, is asking God to place a buffer between us and whatever retribution or retaliatory actions may be directed toward us or those we love in our immediate and extended families, as well as our circle of friends. For those working in service professions, it can expand to your clients, so it is wise to cover them, also. Remember the enemy doesn't employ fairness, so taking "collateral damage" is better than nothing in his opinion.

In our experience, if sufficient resources are available for particularly dangerous threats to the enemy, there are occasions when he will direct that a broken assignment be reissued, technically creating a "new" assignment with another team of unclean spirits. In the same way a volleyball team will rotate players in and out of a match, the enemy will rotate spirits in an attempt to keep us off balance. Limit his ability by using the authority given through the blood of Christ that prevents an assignment from being reissued. "'. . . no weapon that is fashioned against you shall succeed, and you shall refute every tongue that rises against you in judgment. This is the heritage of the servants of the Lord and their vindication from Me, declares the Lord'" (Isaiah 54:17).

Additionally, once a person is delivered from a spirit, the team members still present can become lonely or miss the spirit that has been removed causing a person to feel great loneliness or despair. To prevent this, a Believer can pray that God would make the remaining spirits blind and/or unaware that the deliverance has occurred. We have found this particularly helpful in closing a session when we are in situations where multiple deliverance sessions are needed.

Due to various constraints, such as time, energy, etc., when working with an individual for deliverance, it may be necessary to have multiple sessions. It is extremely important that, at the end of each session, the work that has been done be sealed; otherwise, the person may experience severe attack and go deeper in bondage instead of receiving and experiencing greater freedom.

We have been known to request that God commission angels to be stationed around us, our property, and our family. There have been times when Dallas has been able to see the angels, often three deep, lining our property during and after battle. God is our refuge and our fortress. Psalms 91 is a great passage to have at the ready when preparing for, during, and after the battle.

CHAPTER QUESTIONS

* When might you choose not to proceed in a deliverance session?

* What part of Psalm 91 makes the most impact for you? Why?

Psalm 91:1-8

Safe and Secure

When you sit enthroned under the shadow of Shaddai, you are hidden in the strength of God Most High. Here's how I describe Him: He's the hope that holds me, and the Stronghold to shelter me, the only God for me, and my great Confidence. And He will rescue you from every hidden trap of the enemy, and He will protect you from false accusation and any deadly curse. His massive arms are wrapped around you, protecting you. You can run under His covering of majesty and hide. His arms of faithfulness are a shield keeping you from harm. You will never worry about an attack of demonic forces at night, nor have to fear a spirit of darkness coming against you. Don't fear a thing! Whether by night or by day, demonic danger will not trouble you, nor the powers of evil launched against you. For God will keep you safe and secure; they won't lay a hand on you! Even in a time of disaster with thousands and thousands being killed, you will remain unscathed and unharmed! You will be a spectator as the wicked perish in judgment, for they will be paid back for what they have done!

The Psalms Poetry on Fire, The Passion Translation, Dr. Brian Simmons 2014

WEAPONS AND TECHNIQUES OF WARFARE

As we move further in the process of learning about spiritual warfare, we will be looking at ways in which we engage in battle and techniques, tools, and weapons that we need to be effective in defeating the gates of hell. Remember that our objective in warfare is to free captives from bondage, take back territory lost to the enemy, and to protect territory that is being attacked by the enemy.

LOVE

Jan Sjoerd Pasterkamp says, "The greatest weapon we have against the devil is love" (*Furious Love*, Deluxe Edition. Darren Wilson. Wanderlust Productions, 2010. DVD). In all warfare, we *always* love the *people*, but deal with the destruction the devil is using against them to cause defeat.

When we forget that, we become agents of hurt and destruction, too.

> If I speak in the tongues of men and of angels, but have not love, I am a noisy gong or a clanging cymbal. And if I have prophetic powers, and understand all mysteries and all knowledge, and if I have all faith, so as to remove mountains, but have not love, I am nothing. If I give away all I have, and if I deliver up my body to be burned, but have not love, I gain nothing.
>
> Love is patient and kind; love does not envy or boast; it is not arrogant or rude. It does not insist on its own way; it is not irritable or resentful; it does not rejoice at wrongdoing, but rejoices with the truth. Love bears all things, believes all things, hopes all things, endures all things. Love never ends. . . . So now faith, hope, and love abide, these three; but the greatest of these is love. (1 Corinthians 13:1-8, 13)

When we go into battle, we must go in the love of the Father. God is love (1 John 4:8), and it is because of His great love that we have the power to defeat darkness. For if He hadn't loved us so much, He wouldn't have sent Jesus to be the ultimate sacrifice, providing atonement for our sins and defeating death and hell through His resurrection.

Remember that we battle in the power of the blood of Christ, and we must put on love before we go into battle.

When we are battling the enemy, we do so because of the love of God that is flowing through us for the individuals for whom we are fighting. Sometimes, we can do the greatest damage to the enemy when we simply love on people. Think about how Jesus treated the adulterous woman in John 8:3-11. Her accusers caught her in sin and wanted to destroy her. Jesus, the one who could truly judge her, instead loved her. He saw through the sin and cared for the person. Once she had received forgiveness, she was released to "go and sin no more." Satan is called the accuser of the saints (Revelation 12:10-11). He is constantly catching us in our sins and going before God the Father with accusations of our wrongdoing. Jesus stands in the gap for us and lovingly covers our sins with His blood.

It is easy to accuse, judge, and condemn. Rather than re-enforcing the enemy's position, we are to take that power away from Satan by refusing to condemn and standing in love for people.

PRAYER

We were discussing some of the things God was teaching us and the individual across the table asked, "So what are your tools?" We replied simply, "Prayer." "That's it! That's all you've got?" they asked.

The short answer is, "Yes and no." Prayer is what keeps us connected with our Heavenly Father. Without Him, we can do nothing. There are some tools that can accompany prayer, but we must be connected to the Source for any of them to matter. The thing is, we don't need physical objects, as tools like the other side; no crystal balls, cards (tarot, angel, or otherwise), no crystal jewelry or crucifixes are needed for protection, no Ouija boards, no smoke and mirrors, or imitations. We have access to Truth and Life. That's all we need. We may choose to use anointing oil, but the oil itself has no power.

Prayer is not something to take lightly or to promise but never do. If you find yourself praying over repetitive problems, pray for God to also destroy Satan's assignments and reinforcements. Repetitive prayers might be worry prayers, because you doubt that God will provide. Check your motive behind the continual presentation of the request. There is a difference between begging for a needed provision and demonstrating the sincerity of your heart where a dream or desire is concerned. There is power in speaking Jesus' name (Philippians 2:9-11). "Lord Jesus, I need you. Please come stand right beside me, in front of me, hem me in before and behind. Jehovah--Nissi, My Banner, cover me."

Pray in agreement with God. Pray specifically! Pray without limiting God. The words "just" and "can" may weaken the effectiveness of your prayer. For example, "God can you *just* (fill in request here)?" God is Almighty and *can* do anything He chooses. It's not a question of ability; it's more a question of our faith in this context. The word "just" limits God. What if He wanted to do what you were asking plus something in abundance? You asked for "just" such and such, so He will likely honor the more limited request or petition and not lavish you with the other. He wants you to learn how to pray, so He's willing to withhold the excess.

Ask God to open a space in the Heavens above you, so prayers are not hitting a false ceiling or other impediments placed by the enemy to delay communication between you and the Father. Satan is the "prince of the power of the air" (Ephesians 2:2) and can influence communication. He can also delay the angels from responding (see Daniel 10:12-13). Pray continually. Pray that Satan can't place new assignments based on what is heard. Pray in the Spirit.

Unlike God, Who is omniscient and omnipresent, Satan and his demons are limited to the knowledge that they can obtain. They will listen to our plans and prayers kind of like having our room bugged. If you feel that your plans seem to be known by the enemy, this may be happening to you. The Holy Spirit can block those spies from being able to hear our conversations. Sometimes, we pray a protective bubble over conversations particularly those held in public places.

We need to repent of agreeing that prayer is a socially acceptable, ritualistic, platitude or something cliché that we participate in, or say we will offer on behalf of another, in an awkward situation. Prayer is joining with God, and when we are in His presence, we experience His power. Prayer as God intended, instructed, and gifted it to us is *powerful not pitiful*.

Prayer is talking **with** God; it involves listening to Him. If you need to have a mental image of approaching the Throne or inviting Jesus to join you in a visualized landscape of His creation to make it more personal, do that. He's waiting for you to tell Him how you feel, to ask Him for forgiveness, to ask questions that you have, to ask for direction and guidance, and for you to praise and thank Him.

Prayer is powerful and necessary. Jesus prayed frequently (examples are in Luke 6:12, 9:28 and 11:1, among other times mentioned in the Gospels); and therefore, we need to also be in constant prayer (1 Thessalonians 5:17). When we pray in accordance with the Holy Spirit and faith, the request will be granted (Mark 11:24, 1 John 5:14). "The prayer of a righteous person has great power as it is working (James 5:16b)."

We need to make sure we are walking in purity with God before we move into commanding spirits to leave, or they will have "rights" because of the places of sin and vulnerabilities we have left open. (Acts 19:11-20) We want to be in as strong a place as possible when entering into spiritual warfare, so your unconfessed sins need to be laid bare in front of God with full repentance. While the sin issue does not negate your authority in Christ, it can lessen the fullness of the power available to you and increase the likelihood of resistance from the evil spirits. In other words, God's ability to work is **NOT** impeded by your flaws. Your strength to battle, however, is compromised. Besides, there's no point in trying to cover up a sin. God knows your heart.

Ask God to fill you with His power, strength, energy, peace, and endurance. Pray over yourself, your family, your pets, your property, your reputation, your name, your friends, your boss, etc. Husbands, cover your wives in prayer. As spiritual leaders in your home, you are tasked with looking after the spiritual health and safety of your wife and children.

COMMANDING

There are significant differences in praying and commanding. Praying is only entered into with our Lord and Savior; whereas, commanding is utilizing the authority provided to us through Him to defeat the enemy. Christ's followers **never** pray to the demonic spirits, and we **never** command God.

When commanding the spirits, it can be helpful, but not necessary, to identify the spirit(s) by name. God knows the name(s) and can fortify your battle position by sending angels to escort unnamed spirits out. Spirits and emotions can share names. At times, we command a spirit by how it is manifesting. This is likely due to the intertwining of our tripartite being where body and soul are being impacted together.

When you command, take precaution to cover any animals or pets present, in addition to the people involved. We learned this the hard way. While commanding spirits to depart, including the spirit manifesting as anger, we forgot to protect the dogs present. In the middle of administering inner healing, the dogs were fighting. The instigator had not previously behaved in such an aggressive manner. Upon the realization that we had not protected the animals, we commanded the spirit to leave and forbid it from attaching to another host in its departure. After this experience, we learned to pray for God's protection on all, and then, while commanding the spirits, to use a directive that forbids them from entering pets and other humans, as well as spaces and inanimate objects.

The command may sound like this:

> In the authority of the Name of Jesus and in the Power of His shed blood and resurrection, as a child of God, I renounce (<u>fill in the blank with the specific circumstance(s); vow; judgment; curse</u>)* that allowed Satan and his evil spirits an entry point. I command that all spirits involved in this assignment stand at attention and be frozen and forbidden from manifesting in any way that would be harmful or embarrassing to (<u>fill in with individual's name here</u>). I command that you be unable to communicate with each other or any external spirits in an effort to gain strength. I command that you be mute and unable to continue attacking through thoughts and emotions. I command that all team leaders, team members, named spirits, unnamed spirits, and those known by an alternate name in the spirit realm be gathered together back to back and be bound by the power of the Blood of Christ. I further command that each and every one of these entities should now leave and go directly to (you may choose: the foot of the cross, the lake of fire, Jesus' feet, or any place the Holy Spirit directs at that time—we'll look at those options shortly) without taking any detour and infecting or attaching to another person, another living creature (this

includes pets, animals, and plants), place, or thing/inanimate object.

*Limit yourself to one item at a time. You may repeat this prayer several times during the deliverance process.

We provide this example of a way to command as a guide to learn some of the things that we have found to be helpful in the process. There are no magic formulas for how to command the spirits to be bound and depart. We must follow the direction of the Holy Spirit in all aspects of deliverance including the commands given to the enemy.

We tend to sandwich the commanding portion between prayers. The time of prayer before allows for a time of repentance and forgiveness and strengthening; while the time after allows for praise and thanksgiving for what God has done. The prayers are also a time for listening to further instructions. Since we are operating in God's power and by His direction, it is vital to remain connected with Him. You can also request God's blessing during this time.

As for the choice of location when you are commanding the spirits to leave: if you tend to visualize yourself at the foot of the cross when praying, don't command the spirits to go there; casting them into the lake of fire will remove them, but they will not be confined to hell until the end times when God does so permanently; casting them to the feet of Jesus requires them to acknowledge that He is the King of Kings and Lord of Lords and bow before Him; others choose to instruct them to go where Jesus sends them. Jesus spoke about casting out spirits wandering in dry places (Luke 11:24). Ultimately, you need to be sensitive to the Holy Spirit's direction and follow His instruction for where to send the spirits being banished.

We are more than conquerors (Romans 8:37). We conquer dark spirits in the authority given by God, but we also build up the wounded. Pray that God will dress you in your spiritual armor to enter the battle that is continually all around you, and pray that He will cause Spiritual fruit to abound in your life.

> No, in all these things we are more than conquerors through him who loved us. For I am sure that neither death nor life, nor angels nor rulers, nor things present nor things to come, nor powers, nor height nor depth, nor anything else in all creation, will be able to separate us from the love of God in Christ Jesus our Lord. (Romans 8:37-39)

> But the fruit of the Spirit is love, joy, peace, patience, kindness, goodness, faithfulness, gentleness, self-control; against such things there is no law. (Galatians 5:22-23)

Because the devil doesn't want you to do the work of God, he will do anything in his power to stop you. For example: The two of us set aside a few days to work on the writing of this book, and we went to a cabin in the mountains of Colorado with the nearest neighbor about a half mile away. We prayed for covering and protection before going to the cabin. When we arrived, everything seemed okay. We had prayed for God to send angels to go before us and clean out the space, so that we could be productive. This was shortly after the end of an extremely busy tax season which had required much of Mark's attention and energy. We were both tired but looking forward to the time away and the progress to be made on the training.

We took a little while to settle in, spent some time reading, and then cooked and ate dinner. During this time, our dogs went outside and found a patch of stickers. Our plans had not included spending an hour or more getting a large amount of tiny little stickers out of the dogs' fur and paws. We believe this was an attempt of the enemy to delay, distract, and frustrate us, so we would not accomplish the work that we came to do.

After dinner, our goal was to determine where we were in the material and what holes needed to be filled. We pulled out the computer that had the most recent version of the document, and there were no, and I mean no, none, nada, zero documents on the computer. This was also the computer that Dallas had spent many hours creating a photo montage memory video for our twin daughters' graduation, in addition to being Dallas' work computer that had all of her work-related items on it – QuickBooks data files, group materials, etc., etc. The basic programs were present like when you open a brand-new computer, but there were no additional programs showing that had been loaded and no data files!

As Dallas put it, "It was like getting punched in the gut. I was just in disbelief that they could really be gone."

After a few minutes of panic and some text messages with Mark's computer guy, we still had no data files. We did the only thing we knew to do – cried out to God. Ok, there was some other crying as well, but we digress. We poured ourselves out to our Lord, asking for Him to fix the computer. And you know what? He did _not_ fix the computer!

Instead, He told us to handle the situation! Us? He's GOD, we're just people, and not very computer savvy people at that. But He gave us both the insight that we needed to take command. After a brief faith check, Mark picked up the computer, and we did what we knew to do. We started to command the computer to reveal the data files. We commanded the evil one to give them back and unhide them. When we instruct the enemy in the power of Jesus, he must obey our commands, because they are tied to his submission to Christ's authority. He revealed the files. As Mark scrolled to the end of the document to verify the page count, he read the very last statement Dallas had written on the page which said, "It really is war, and the enemy doesn't fight fair."

Almost immediately after the files were revealed, the wind outside became extremely fierce. It sounded angry with persistent eerie howling. It seemed the demons wanted to show their disgust with being defeated, but we are more than conquerors in Christ Jesus.

Earlier that day, our pastor preached on the favor of God in his sermon. Dallas said at one point, "This does not feel like favor. Lord, please show me how this is favor." She was right; it didn't feel like favor in the midst of it. When you realize that the favor of God is not just a blessing and easy life, then you can start to see His favor even in the difficult times. He does not promise ease. In fact, Jesus said that we should take up our cross and follow Him (see Matthew 10:38 and Luke 9:23). Taking up a cross is not easy. It is painful, difficult, and extremely unpleasant; however, the favor of God is always good.

We know for some of you, this is outside of your comfort zone and frame of reference. How do we take a painful, difficult experience and call it good? We should focus on

the outcome of what God is accomplishing through the experience! Today, we can see that through this experience we have grown through the process, and we have another lesson to teach. There you have it, God's favor.
We were praying that God would give us the material to write and complete the training. He was simply answering our prayer – just not in the way we expected.

A couple of lessons that came out of this experience. First is that when you set out to do great things in obedience to God, there will be points at which the evil one will attempt to distract, sidetrack, hinder, and anything else to stop you. You have to stay focused on Jesus Christ and be obedient to His instruction. You must stand strong in the strength of the Lord and fight.

The second lesson is that God wants us to do our part. That means that He is equipping and gifting us to take charge of the evil one's interruptions and attacks. Praying is always good, but there are times when we have to engage in warfare beyond prayer by commanding the demonic spirits. As Dallas' grandma used to say, "You learn to do by doing." In God's boot camp, He has you engage, so He can continue to train and mature you.

IDENTIFYING SPIRITS

As you command, *sometimes* it is necessary to identify and name the spirit you are addressing. How do you identify them? They may identify themselves, God may choose to "word drop" their name(s) in the form of Divine Knowledge, and you may not need a name. We have found that you can command the spirits to identify themselves; however, if it is a lying spirit, you can't believe what it says. This can be a frustrating process. We have learned not to allow them to sidetrack us with the need for a specific name.

It is also possible that you do not need to address them by name. The spirits can externally influence by causing frustration, taking a long time to comply, and can harass if you become wrapped up in needing to know all the names and details. God knows the names and details. Ask Him to speak them out into the spirit realm instead of getting bogged down here. We have been known to issue a command identifying an evil spirit by the behavior it is causing rather than an actual name.

Some enemy spirits masquerade as emotions. This can be confusing, because we need God to help us discern if it is an emotional response that He created us to have or if it is an attack of the enemy. When identifying and commanding enemy spirits, make sure to say, ". . . named and unnamed, and those known by alternative names in the spirit world."

We do this, because they like to mess with us by not complying based on the fact that we didn't actually address them and tell them to leave.

DREAMS AND VISIONS

Dreams can also be a part of warfare. Some are legitimate dreams while you sleep, and others are visions during waking hours. We have experienced both. Dreams can be warnings, brief glimpses of the future, reassurance from God, or they can be an attack from the enemy to increase fear or suffering causing one to abandon the battle post. Ask the Father for discernment and wisdom.

The first time Dallas prayed in tongues was in a dream. At the time, she discounted it as an unknown foreign language rather than understanding that she was praying over someone in the Spirit. It was only later when she was introduced to the man she was praying over in her dream that she realized this was a divine appointment even as she slept.

We have found it important to document our dreams. As soon as possible, write down as many of the details of the dream as you can recall. Some find it easiest to write the dream as a narrative; while others prefer to use bullet points. Date the entry. God will likely remind you of a dream at some point in the future, and it is helpful to be able to go back and review the notes.

Some dreams are for the present and some for the future. You may receive dreams that are specific only to you; while others may need to be shared with someone else. Dream interpretation is beyond the scope of this book.

PRAISE

It's been said that there are only two times to praise God: when you feel like it and when you don't. That means we are to praise God and be grateful regardless of the outcome. The enemy spirits want you to focus on the dire circumstances and only praise God when He responds with relief, interventions, signs, and wonders. They want to totally distract you from any praise of God. You are praising God for His being, regardless of what He does or doesn't do. Eventually, if they can't get you to move your focus from God to them, they will likely become frustrated and give up in that area of your life.

Keep a blessing/miracle journal. It will help you remember the times God has stepped in and accomplished a huge work in your life. It will help pull you through the tough times of struggle.

WAYS TO PRAISE

Call out the Names of God the Father, Son, and Holy Spirit. Call out His attributes and character traits. Pull out the Bible and make a list of His Names that are meaningful to you.

Thank Him. You can praise Him through offering thanksgiving for all the things you can recall that He has done for you. You can thank Him for the things He has completed and the things He will do. This is simply a separation of gratitude and faith. A heart of gratitude thanks God for what one has already experienced; while faith thanks Him for a resolution and intervention that is within His character but has yet to materialize. Thank Him that through Him, Satan and all the enemy spirits are already defeated.

Use songs and Scripture to praise. Dallas finds it easier to recall Scripture that she has learned in the context of a melody. Maybe this applies to you as well. Sing, hum, read Scripture aloud or sing aloud to a melody running in your head.

Play a musical instrument as praise. You can use traditional instruments and play in solo or ensemble formats. You can play a tambourine along with a song recorded by another artist, sound a shofar, or learn a new instrument that you consecrate to the Lord to use solely in praise and worship of Him.

Use postures of praise. Stand with your arms raised, kneel, or lie prostrate on the floor. Perhaps, you will find that in your praise, you also incorporate worshipful dance or waving flags. Flags are used to enhance worship and can be used to engage in deliverance and warfare. They are an instrument and as such should be used at the prompting of the Holy Spirit with reverence and skill.

> While the Lord desires that we enjoy His gifts, He would have us know we were created first for His pleasure. At the end of this age, the Lord will have a people whose singular purpose for living is to please God. In them, God finds His own reward for creating man. They are His worshipers. The Lord takes them further and through more conflicts than other men. Outwardly, they often seem "smitten of God and afflicted" (Isaiah 53:4). Yet they are beloved to God. When they are crushed, like the petals of a flower, they exude a worship, the fragrance of which is so beautiful and rare that angels weep in quiet awe at their surrender. (Frangipane, F. *The Three Battlegrounds,* Pg. 93)

CHAPTER QUESTIONS

* Of the weapons and techniques, which one stood out to you? Why?

* How does 1 Corinthians 13:1-3 apply to spiritual warfare?

* Write out a commanding statement for your personal use.

HOW SATAN WORKS

Satan works through guilt and shame, markers, triggers, manipulation, intimidation, assignments, and protective curses. The Bible tells us that Satan is a master of deception, and he knows the words of God. He works to make things look pretty or safe that truly are not. He can do this subtly, or he can go out of his way to generate an illusion that is astonishing. We see this for the first time in the Garden of Eden, when as a serpent, Satan says to Eve, "Did God really say that, or does He just want to maintain His position and title of Lord?" (Genesis 3:1, 5). Okay, that's a loose paraphrase, but you get the idea. Satan made the forbidden tree of the Knowledge of Good and Evil look appealing, but what it really brought about was guilt and shame. These emotions made it so that Adam and Eve hid from God, and they make it hard for us today to come into God's presence. These emotions become our prison, and Satan likes to keep us there. Remember the adage: not everything that glitters is gold. Don't be deceived!

> "You are of your father the devil, and your will is to do your father's desires. He was a murderer from the beginning, and does not stand in the truth, because there is no truth in him. When he lies, he speaks out of his own character, for he is a liar and the father of lies." (John 8:44)

Once he has you trapped, he keeps you there with deeply seeded emotions like anger, guilt, and shame. Pride and greed are also extremely strong emotions in which the enemy likes us to dwell. Likely, he has accused you of things for so long, that you have managed to completely believe the lies he is feeding you. It may have been long enough, that he can turn the rage, guilting, and shaming over to you, because he knows you will continue to reinforce those false accusations yourself. How convenient; he's convinced you to accept these lies and guilt and live out of a false identity contrary to what God created you to be. This means you are living a life of defeat, and he no longer needs to worry about you impacting the world for God's Kingdom.

> "Satan wants to attack your mind, your thoughts, your feelings, and your emotions. He realizes that this is the easiest way to make inroads. The devil wants to corrupt your emotions, especially, because they can flip a negative coin in your soul. Emotions are more easily manipulated than cognitive thoughts are. Love becomes lust. Anger becomes

vengeance. Fear becomes incapacitation. Sorrow becomes uncontrollable grief." (Larson, B. *Demon Proofing Prayers*, Pp. 61-62)

He utilizes manipulation with great skill. In perverting things that are good, imitating what God created, offering perceived benefits, exerting assignments, and instructing that protective curses be performed, Satan exercises a great deal of control. Satan does not create anything good but rather imitates and warps that which God originally created. After all, he is the "father of lies," and that is his character (John 8:44). Such exploits leave us with a mutated representation of what God intended to be pure and lovely.

"And no wonder, for even Satan disguises himself as an angel of light. So it is no surprise if his servants, also, disguise themselves as servants of righteousness. Their end will correspond to their deeds." (2 Corinthians 11:14-15)

Perceived benefits are like seeing a beautifully wrapped package and beginning to unwrap it only to find a bomb inside. In other words, you thought you were getting one thing by entering an agreement with him, and he gave you something else. Sneaky, huh?

Think about those that are enamored and allured by fortune and fame. In their pursuit of either or both, they will often agree to forsake values that they once held. They may also continue to look for relief or escape through various addictions. The monetarily rich may someday realize that they are poor in relationships, and the famous may be ill-esteemed when their reputations precede them. This wasn't what they thought they were getting, nor what they hoped would satisfy their desires and longings. Satan will always provide an inferior substitute, or more than one, to fill the void that God created within us so that we would seek after Him.

GUILT AND SHAME

There are some emotions that are easily confused with each other. We find that this is often the case with guilt and conviction. Let's look at the difference between the two.

The motive behind guilt is to weigh one down. Guilt is perpetual unless it is cut off and removed. Guilt never allows for repentance, repair, or restoration. Guilt keeps a record of wrongs. When it shifts from being an emotional response into the demonic realm, it can often allow you to become your own tormentor, because you have believed a lie and agreed to it. The enemy no longer needs to expend resources or energy targeting that area for you. There are some Christians that espouse the thought that Believers "need" guilt. To be fair, it seems they are attempting to differentiate between good guilt and bad guilt; however, because guilt is oppressive in nature, we must still wholeheartedly disagree with the concept that anyone needs guilt.

What we need is conviction. In conviction, there is still an awareness and recognition of wrongdoing, sin. Even though the consequences of such behaviors are not necessarily cancelled or removed, God always provides a way for us to be reconciled and brought back into the fullness of relationship through the process of forgiveness. Conviction, while uncomfortable, is motivated by love and restoration to bring one back into right standing. There is no condemnation in such a process unlike with a pattern of guilt (Romans 8:1).

There is a HUGE difference between guilt or shame and conviction. Guilt and shame keep us tied to past failures and short comings with no possibility of personal restoration or reconciliation with others. Guilt and shame are not useful disciplinary tools, because they are oppressive. Shame is tied to humiliation over behavior or performance. Professional journals are publishing studies suggesting that humiliation can often be more harmful than physical attacks.

Conviction, on the other hand, offers the opportunity to acknowledge and turn from the sin, failure, and/or short coming. It offers the ability to learn from a mistake and repair misunderstandings. In short, Satan offers defeat through guilt and shame, and God offers hope and love through conviction.

PRIDE

Satan offers status and prestige through pride. Pride, in its basest form, is putting our opinions before God's will, and it is what caused Satan to fall from Heaven (Proverbs 16:18, Isaiah 14:12-15; Revelation 12:7-9). The devil still uses pride to inflict pain, misery, and destruction; although at the time of the initial agreement, there is a perceived benefit of gained influence.

There are many ways pride can manifest. Personally, one may begin to gain public notoriety and begin to feel entitled, or professionally, one may begin to feel superior to all others around them. In the spiritual realm, pride can be tied to a spirit of religion.

This was present in Jesus' day with the Pharisees and Sadducees. The religious spirit attempts to convince us that if we do all the right things, we will earn our way into God's good graces and reserve a spot in Heaven. The Bible says, "For by grace you have been saved through faith. And this is not your own doing; it is the gift of God, not a result of works, so that no one may boast" (Ephesians 2:8-9). Jesus is the only way into Heaven (John 14:6).

This same unholy spirit works the other angle of, "If you don't always live an upright life, you will forever be condemned." The Bible says, "There is therefore now no condemnation for those who are in Christ Jesus" (Romans 8:1).

The religious spirit exercises control by creating division in the body of Christ through a multitude of denominational beliefs that become divisions rather than distinctions. It can persuade an individual to vehemently defend God, which presumes God is not capable of defending Himself, or encourage a life of legalism and judgment.

Jesus said there were many things that He could point out and condemn, but that He would hold His tongue simply because God did not instruct Him to voice those concerns (John 8:26). Choosing to avoid judgment weakens a religious spirit.

Blame is often a counterpart of pride. When approached with having done something wrong, some will instinctively turn the conversation to blame on another. "I did that, because of what they did." Honest self-examination is difficult when a spirit of pride is present.

God says the humble have a special place in His heart, and He esteems them (Proverbs 3:34, James 4:6, 1 Peter 5:5-6). When we approach our differences with humility, we come much closer to a place of unity with our brothers and sisters in Christ.

In the context of spiritual warfare and deliverance work, a humble spirit can hear direction from God. It becomes very dangerous territory if we begin to assume, "I know what I'm doing. I've got this." Formulas and manmade systems may work for a time, but they do not honor God.

MARKERS

In Satanic Ritual Abuse (SRA), it is common for Christian symbols to become perverted even to the point of having a man dressed like Christ "hanging" on a cross, coming down from the cross and raping children. Victims of abuse whether SRA or other modalities are marked by Satan for easier identification of vulnerabilities later in life. Again, this is a perversion of what God created when He placed a mark on Cain after he killed his brother Abel. The mark from God was a protective measure, so no one would kill Cain (see Genesis 4:8-16).

Other instances of God using markings are found in Exodus 12:7, 12-13, when the blood marked the door of the Israelites and the Angel of Death passed over them, and in

Ezekiel 9 when God instructed that the righteous individuals that were grieved over the sin in Jerusalem be marked on their foreheads. This marking would indicate that they were to be passed over and protected from death.

In contrast to God's protective mark, markers (also called markings) placed by the enemy for unholy and evil purposes are places of vulnerability. Satan likes to mark those that have been abused sexually, involved in the occult whether willingly or unwillingly (including, but not limited to, SRA), those that have been adulterous, and those who participate in most habitual sin behaviors. The markings make these individuals easier targets, because the demons know exactly where to go for the weakest point.

Unfortunately, many people, especially in today's culture, have chosen to put physical markings on their bodies. Tattoos and piercings can be doors by which evil spirits gain an entry point to a person. The symbolism of tattoos, whether Christian, demonic, or seemingly benign, is very real in the spirit realm. In some cases, tattoos and piercings are purposely cursed to invite demonic presence. Remember, the demonic spirit world looks for legal rights. If the tattoo or piercing artist attaches a curse to their work or the jewelry adorning your body, you carry that curse wherever you go. We are not saying that all tattoos and piercings are cursed, but there is a significant presence of demonic activity associated with tattoos and piercings.

We often pray that God will either cover the marking so that it is hidden under the blood of Christ, or we pray it be completely removed in the spiritual realm, so that the vulnerability no longer remains. Markers, targets, and tracking devices . . . all these terms are used to represent basically the same idea with subtle nuances. With tracking devices, we ask that they be completely destroyed and disabled.

TRIGGERS

Satan's marks are specifically designed to track you for destruction and torment. In Satanic Ritual Abuse, triggers are purposely programmed or implanted. Triggers are meant to cause the person agony and demand compliance. They can come in the form of people, places, things, sounds, smells, words, etc. The trigger becomes a cue for the person to reengage with the evil world rather than leaving and finding deliverance and freedom.

Triggers are cues that set off a preprogrammed response emotionally and physically. Those who suffer from PTSD from combat experience can relate to being triggered by a car backfiring or surrounding vegetation reminding them of being in the jungle; space, or a limitation thereof, may trigger a response of claustrophobia; a smell may bring back a flood of memories; a spoken word, phrase, or sound can initiate a predetermined response; and a date on the calendar can, likewise, function as a trigger (i.e., occult high days, birthdays, anniversaries, etc.).

Hypnosis is a way in which people can become vulnerable to triggers being placed. While the individual is in a subconscious state, they are at the complete control and direction of the hypnotist. Christians should never allow anyone outside of God to have such control over them.

Satan actively employs triggers to keep those with ties to the occult from breaking free. There is a real threat on people's physical lives when they attempt to leave the occult. Satan would rather arrange to have them "disappear" than to have them inform the world of his deplorable practices. Such individuals, and those trying to protect and disciple them, report being stalked unmercifully and being on hyper alert, because their lives are in jeopardy. Once they are saved, they can identify with the Apostle Paul when he said that in both death and life, Christ would be glorified (Philippians 1:21). Talk about making it impossible for your tormenter to win with that attitude.

MANIPULATION

Satan is also a master manipulator. He perverts and imitates the things of God; while he offers perceived benefits that never seem to materialize. Abusers know how to manipulate and/or groom their intended victims. They do so by being super charming and saying things that are enticing or flattering. Once their victim is bonded or connected to them, all bets are off and the charm, promises, and flattery quickly disappear. Satan is the ultimate abuser. He wants you to be so insecure in your faith that despair can take over. If he can't have your spirit, he will take your soul (remember that is your thoughts and emotions) and physical body to a place of destruction (1 Peter 5:8).

Satan's demons and evil spirits also depend on deception, manipulation, and trickery to maintain a presence. These devices assist them in being able to remain in a host or to continue tormenting the host externally for as long as possible. They do this by hiding. Sometimes, this is done in a more physical realm which requires that the Believer look in the physical realm with spiritual eyes, but it occurs more often in the spiritual realm.

We have seen this happen when a spirit tries to deflect attention away from itself by saying that it didn't permit the exact behavior of its own name and function. Other ways this has manifested is when the spirit uses an alternate name or alias. They feel they have a right to stay, simply because you didn't identify them correctly. We have learned to begin commanding by identifying the name we instinctively perceive which sometimes is given as a word of knowledge from the Lord.

INTIMIDATION

One of Satan's tools that he uses regularly is intimidation. Much like a bully on the playground, he looks, acts, and is mean. He'll call you names and tell you that you aren't strong enough or smart enough or you don't know enough. He still operates like when he tempted Jesus in the desert (Matthew 4:1-11 and Luke 4:1-13). He will quote Scriptures, often twisted or out of context to misrepresent the true meaning. His goal is to get you to think that he is more powerful and convince you that you will not win a battle with him.

These are all lies, because we are not battling in our own strength, intelligence or knowledge. We are battling in the power of the blood of Jesus Christ. As a child of the King of kings and Lord of lords, we have all the power and authority bestowed upon us by Him to win every battle. Do not allow Satan to intimidate you!

ASSIGNMENTS

Assignments are exactly what the name implies. Satan wants a certain task accomplished, so he makes an assignment against a person, a group of people, families, organizations, etc.

Those called into ministry are often targets of assignments. This is a long-standing pattern and one worth noting, so you can pray more specific coverings over your pastors and leaders. Think about it. If you take out one individual, it has minimal effect in a battle, but if you take out several, that can become a feather in your hat so to speak. The enemy wants to destroy, or at least immobilize, as many Christians as he possibly can, so he will most often attack the leaders.

Ministers often find that beyond themselves, their families or congregations can come under specific enemy assignments. Church planters and missionaries attempting to start new churches or reach previously unreached people groups are a huge threat to the enemy. We happened to find ourselves in the crosshairs when we moved to Colorado to church plant and pastor. The assignment had elements of burnout, failure, rejection, and death in it. We were not aware of the depths of the assignment at the time; we simply knew that we needed some assistance. In retrospect, we believe that those whom we asked for help colluded with the enemy's forces in the assignment, perhaps unknowingly. Because we were not yet aware of how to engage in spiritual warfare, we were not praying or commanding against these things. Even after operating in such a state of naivety, we have found God to be faithful to redeem the results of the assignment. In other words, what the enemy, or simply other people, meant for evil, God used for good (Genesis 50:20). God works all things together for the good of those who love Him (Romans 8:28).

Without God's intervention, assignments remain in play until the task is accomplished even if certain dark entities are cast out. The limited authority that God allows Satan for a time permits the enemy to utilize his power unless it is commanded to come under that of Christ and His shed blood (Job 1:12, 2:6). Because demons are working as a team, or teams, to accomplish this one task, the evil spirits will rotate in and out much like players on a volleyball team. Assignments can be broken off in their entirety through God's authority. If you have permitted the assignment through a sin issue, repentance of the sin is required. We see examples of prophets repenting of the sins of the nation (Daniel, Jeremiah), so it is possible that you need to repent of the sins of your ancestors, leaders, or nation. Following His forgiveness, ask God to destroy the assignment for you.

Assignments are one of the tactics used against individuals and entire family lines. Sometimes, this manifests as a generational curse. While God is a loving God, He is also a just God. Since He is the same yesterday, today, and tomorrow (Hebrews 13:8), the love, grace, and mercy do not replace His just nature. There is a consequence for all sin (Romans 6:23). God will not look on sin in approval; therefore, it is possible that the sins of the father (for many generations back) will be visited upon the following generations (Exodus 20:5-6), unless the curse is broken off through Christ. The curses God placed on Adam and Eve still impact us today. There are thorns and weeds that make it harder to produce crops, and childbirth is still a painful process. Other assignments may come in the form of addiction, divorce, suicide, mental illness, or abuse.

When you identify a destructive pattern in your own life or family line, determine if it is a bad habit or an assignment. If the latter, then break it off as assignments typically continue until they are broken in the power of God. In dealing with assignments, you may find that an intentional change in behavior is necessary in addition to renouncing the assignment.

Assignments have been issued against the church, too. In gaining just enough exposure to the concepts of spiritual warfare but not fully understanding how to participate in that realm, the assignment of ineffectiveness has taken hold. The church has become inoculated and immune to seeing the ramifications of spiritual warfare, because it has had or heard about just enough to feel the members won't be impacted if they keep their heads down and check all the boxes. Not only is there an air of ineffectiveness, but there is also an evidence of fear of the unknown and a fear of the manifestations of the Holy Spirit, as well as dark spirits. Since when was God more interested in a complete checklist and a complete understanding that furnishes control than an attitude of obedience and seeking after all of Him? God is much more interested in our devotion and pure hearts (1 Samuel 15:22).

Remember, we operate within an authority structure, because God designed authority and hierarchy. When we break off a destructive pattern in our family, He permits us the privilege of repenting on behalf of ancestors and leaders, as well as covering future generations, such as our children and grandchildren. Ultimately, you must ask God how much influence and authority He permits you within the context of relationships. This is a result of each person having a will to execute personal values and decisions.

Protective assignments are a secondary umbrella to keep the original from being completely lifted. Think of the original assignment as a false ceiling. Even if you demolish the false ceiling, you are still limited by the other ceiling. Protective assignments are common with generational assignments particularly if there has been involvement in the occult.

Satan is the father of lies (John 8:44) and has come to steal, kill, and destroy (John 10:10). He will use whatever means possible to keep us from health, holiness, and a right relationship with God. We need to be wise as serpents and gentle as doves (Matthew 10:16); therefore, we should be aware of the evil one's schemes (2 Corinthians 2:11) and remove from our lives unnecessary opportunities and advantages that he can use against us.

CHAPTER QUESTIONS

* What are some tactics that the enemy has used against you?

* What markers or triggers do you need to cover in the blood of Christ?

* What assignments can you identify against you or your family?

THE PLAYERS

If you're going to war, you need to know the players. Those that understand their opponent fare better in times of war.

There is a hierarchy and a lowerarchy, if you will. C.S. Lewis coined the term lowerarchy in his book, *The Screwtape Letters*, and we have adopted its use. The use of hierarchy represents the holy side, and the use of lowerarchy represents the evil side.

> "Satan appoints ruling spirits or strongmen over every principality or control area. The major ones rule from the mid-heavens, and a hierarchy [lowerarchy] exists in which other ruling spirits control each level in descending order. It ends with a ruling spirit in each individual. It is similar to the chain of command adopted by earthly armies. The generals sit on thrones at the top level while the sergeants at the bottom control the demons that occupy a stronghold in a person." (Ing, R. *Spiritual Warfare,* Pg. 20)

Within the hierarchy, there is the Trinity: God the Father, Jesus Christ the Son, and the Holy Spirit. Each of the three is wholly God, but each has a different function. Each personhood of God has many names. The angels are also present within the hierarchy with varying levels of angels being indicated in the Bible.

Within the lowerarchy, are Satan, principalities, demons, and unclean spirits. Other entities within this structure include strongmen, princes, rulers, and authorities. Each has varying levels of power and scope of operating (Daniel 10:13, Matthew 12:43, Mark 1:23-24, John 12:31, 1 Peter 5:8, Revelation 12:9). *For the purposes of this book, evil spirits, spiritual forces of darkness, the enemy or dark angels/spirits are a generalized term to encompass all entities of the lowerarchy.*

Satan is known by various names such as Lucifer, Abaddon, deceiver, father of lies and even the angel of light (John 8:44, 2 Corinthians 11:14). In the latter case, Satan is disguised in an attempt to successfully entice the person in his presence. One should be suspicious of any angel presenting itself in the appearance of a female form or a form which is docile and winged as the "traditional" decorative notion we have grown accustomed to seeing.

Modern day artistic representations remind us that there is an angelic realm. In that sense, I don't think it's wrong to have them around. It **IS** wrong to worship them in any way. Scriptures indicate that angels are masculine in their spiritual existence, and when they take on human form in the Bible, it is that of a man. God is Sovereign. He may choose to have an angel take on any form He wishes to accomplish His will, but I would encourage you to test any spirit or angel serving as a messenger if it presents itself in the culturally accepted form. Biblical accounts of angels describe them as having many eyes and wings, as well as being a presence that evokes fear and requires reassurance. (Genesis 18:1-2, 1 Chronicles 21:27, Job 4:15-16, Luke 1:28-30, Revelation 4:8).

Spirits can be arranged into teams, so they have more strength. Collusion between teams can be present for added enforcement; therefore, when you are dealing with spiritual attack, you need to be mindful to address team leaders and team members. Be sure to cut off the ability to communicate with each other in any manner especially for the purpose of gaining strength.

SPECIFIC SPIRITS

There are numerous dark spirits that could be included and discussed; however, that is not the focus of this work. We have deliberately decided to discuss a few briefly just to give you a glimpse of how they typically act. Other authors have gone into greater detail, and to the extent that God wants you to research, we encourage you to seek out those additional resources.

There are a few specific dark spirits that particularly enjoy wreaking havoc in the lives of Christians; Belial, Leviathan, Jezebel, Ahab, as well as those that lend their powers to Freemasonry and the occult to name a few. The Jezebel spirit shows herself frequently in the need to control or in sexual desires and works to destroy churches; while the Ahab spirit leads people to give up their authority, effectively making them powerless and impotent.

Freemasonry and its feeder organizations worship Satan and have morbid rituals that are faithfully observed. Because these organizations are secretive, they lure in unsuspecting individuals. We use a very specific and in depth prayer when dealing with individuals who report having any personal or familial contact with such organizations. These are not simply social clubs. *They are dangerous*, and participation gives Satan an entry point not only to you but to your entire family line. We should never commit or even participate in any spiritual organization that is not based solely on the worship of the one true God (Father, Son, and Holy Spirit).

BELIAL

Belial, in Hebrew *beliyyaal*, is defined as worthless. In the Old Testament, Belial is mentioned frequently in the King James Version. In modern English versions, Belial is typically translated as "worthless men" or "sons of lawlessness" (i.e., 1 Samuel 2:12, 2 Samuel 16:7, 1 Kings 21:13). Belial is used as a proper name in 2 Corinthians 6:15 where Paul says, "What accord has Christ with Belial."

Belial is a general spirit of lawlessness turning the hearts of men away from the Lord. Belial commands addiction spirits which include greed, the addiction to wealth, spirits of infirmity or sickness, lust, perversion, and reprobate spirits, such as those dealing in rejection and worthlessness. These spirits then have at their disposal other dark spirits such as unrighteousness, sexual immorality, wickedness, rebellion, death, and destruction, which then command lower and more specifically targeted demons.

LEVIATHAN

Leviathan is deceitful. Job talks about Leviathan in chapter 3 as something to be cursed and in chapter 41 as a sea creature that is not easily caught. Isaiah 27:1 says, "In that day the LORD with his hard and great and strong sword will punish Leviathan the fleeing serpent, Leviathan the twisting serpent, and he will slay the dragon that is in the sea." We see in Psalms 74 that Leviathan has many heads. The multiple heads can sometimes be seen in multiple personalities of a person.

Some deliverance workers call this entity the twister spirit. Leviathan will use twisting spirits to accomplish his goals. A twister spirit is one that takes a truth and distorts it to mean something else.

Leviathan will weave himself into a person's life in such a way that he is not easily identified and removed. During a deliverance session, God permitted Mark to see into the spirit realm. He could see an evil spirit coming out in a fashion similar to a corkscrew, since it had interwoven through the person's mind and being. Multiple false beliefs had been adopted by the person, such that their identity was distorted. We had to remove the false beliefs in order for the individual to realize their true identity in Christ.

JEZEBEL

Jezebel is infamous for her manipulation and abuse of power. She was married to Ahab but she did not submit to his authority in any way. Her name mirrors her character, as it means un-husbanded. We refer to this dark spirit in the feminine form because of its namesake rather than using it to denote gender.

"A Jezebel spirit defiles everything it touches. That which is holy becomes vile. People will begin to leave a church, not knowing why; simply feeling compelled to go as if they could feel the impending darkness" (Jackson, J. *Unmasking the Jezebel Spirit*, Pg. 14).

We have dealt with the Jezebel spirit not only in individuals, but also in church leadership. The result in the latter has been division and eventual death of the church if she wasn't overcome. Unless this spirit is cast out and the individual repents of the sin that allowed her in, that person needs to be removed from any position of leadership. *Remember that while the Jezebel spirit is referred to in the feminine, the individual impacted may be either male or female.* We must follow Christ's instructions in Matthew 18:15-17 and Paul's instructions to Timothy when administering required discipline (1 Timothy 5:19-21).

Jezebel is a very strong spirit, and she has many spirits subject to her command. Typically, you will not find all of these spirits present in the same individual, but rarely will you find Jezebel without other spirits present. She uses the other spirits to hide and protect herself. We've mistakenly thought we had provided deliverance to find out that we had simply dealt with the lesser spirits.

Jesus tells the church in Thyatira to stay away from and no longer tolerate Jezebel. He also associates her with the "deep things of Satan."

> Revelation 2:20-25: "But I have this against you, that you tolerate that woman Jezebel, who calls herself a prophetess and is teaching and seducing my servants to practice sexual immorality and to eat food sacrificed to idols. I gave her time to repent, but she refuses to repent of her sexual immorality. Behold, I will throw her onto a sickbed, and those who commit adultery with her I will throw into great tribulation, unless they repent of her works, and I will strike her children dead. And all the churches will know that I am he who searches mind and heart, and I will give to each of you according to your works. But to the rest of you in Thyatira, who do not hold this teaching, who have not learned what some call the deep things of Satan, to you I say, I do not lay on you any other burden. Only hold fast what you have until I come."

AHAB

Jezebel and Ahab most often appear together in a couple or two people that are close. A person with the Ahab spirit is generally passive in the relationship but very protective of the person with the Jezebel spirit. With the Jezebel spirit in control, the Ahab spirit can enjoy the luxury of irresponsibility.

Sometimes, the Ahab and Jezebel spirits will be shared in a couple (married or close friends), appearing (manifesting) in whichever individual is more beneficial for a given situation, trading hosts as necessary. It is rare to have a Jezebel spirit operating independent of an Ahab spirit.

"The spirit of Ahab symbolizes the abdication of authority, or at the very least, passive authority" (Jackson, J. *Unmasking the Jezebel Spirit*, Pg. 12).

Individuals with the Ahab spirit tend to be selfish and needy. They use other people for their benefit regardless of the other person's feelings or integrity of the truth. You may find a deep childhood wound of neglect present with the Ahab spirit, since it tends to have elements of rejection and mind control at its disposal.

The biblical account of Ahab and Jezebel can be found in 1 Kings 16-19 and 21; and 2 Kings 9.

CHAPTER QUESTIONS

* How does the understanding of the hierarchy and lowerarchy affect your method of warfare?

* How does the Bible describe angels?

WALKING IN VICTORY

When studying any topic, it is easy to get into the mindset that it applies to everything in life. We need to realize not every difficult circumstance that happens is spiritual warfare, yet we also need to be aware when the spiritual is present in the physical. This requires constant communication with the Lord, primarily listening, not talking.

Whether child or adult, all of us make choices which impact our lives and those around us. Living with consequences of choices is not always equal to spiritual warfare. God disciplines those He loves, and at times, a natural consequence becomes a part of that process. Sometimes children act like children and noises are just two physical objects bumping.

Early in our journey of learning about the spirit realm, we were on high alert for anything potentially related to warfare, especially in our home. As we were sitting at the table talking about spiritual principles we were learning, we started hearing rattling glass. Dallas looked at Mark; other than returning her eye contact, he didn't respond. Dallas went into combat mode commanding the spirits responsible for banging the glass together to cease, because she thought the sound was meant to disrupt the conversation or create a fearful response. The glass kept rattling. This time when Dallas looked at Mark, he said, "You know, Honey, sometimes noise is just glass banging against glass due to the physical vibrations of the refrigerator. I regularly separate those, so the noise won't irritate you."

The Western church tends to view spiritual warfare through the lenses of extremes on a continuum; deciding to ignore and downplay the activity of the evil one and his minions or to over-emphasize this aspect of the Christian walk seeing an evil spirit under every rock. As Christians, we aren't truthfully able to say, "the devil made me do it," as a way of excusing either position which exist as opposing values on the continuum, but we can accurately state that it is possible for the demonic to influence our behavior at times. A battle is raging for our hearts and minds, we must engage in the battle as the Lord instructs.

We were born into the battle, and it rages whether we choose to engage or not (2 Corinthians 10:3-6). Some have questioned why engaging in warfare must be so complicated and express a desire for it to be simple. Others have found it intriguing and take pleasure in watching the demons respond to their commands which Jesus warns against (Luke 10:20). Some find themselves desiring to live in the light rather than the darkness that consumes their lives, but they stop short of engaging in the battle into which they were born. Employing an "ignorance is bliss" attitude simply does not excuse you from the impact of the battle that rages.

The enemy wants to cause as much havoc and destruction as he can. Hollywood portrays deliverance (sometimes called exorcism) as messy, often with great opposition and physical manifestation by the spirit. While there are times in which the manifestation is allowable or even needed as discussed below, we find that for most, it is best to command the spirit not to cause any physical discomfort or harm to the individual. We are in a spiritual battle, not a physical one, so we primarily don't allow the physical manifestations. Deliverance is the work of the Holy Spirit. If He instructs you to allow the manifestation, it serves His purpose. Our best advice is to always listen to the direction of the Holy Spirit. If needed, you can also limit the evil spirit's expression of displeasure by forbidding them to disrupt objects in the physical, e.g., knocking things off walls or shelves, making a mess of whatever is available, etc. We have been known to command spirits to be bound to a chair to provide an extra level of protection to the individual, as well as ourselves.

Permitting a visual manifestation may be allowable or even beneficial if you are working in a culture where the spiritual is frequently manifested in the physical. The individual that is being delivered, as well as those observing, may need to see a physical response from the spirits, as they are kicked out to believe that something was done. Be sure to care for the physical needs of an individual as much as possible. Provide a trash can for one vomiting, keep them from hitting their head, remove furnishings and decorative items that could be used as "weapons." Again, the Holy Spirit will provide guidance on what is permitted and what is not.

Sometimes there is more to be discovered and learned through the process than in the result. We are on a journey with the Lord. As with a physical journey, there will be hills to climb, mountaintops to celebrate, valleys to go through and rivers to cross. Not everything is easy, and certainly not everything works the way we planned or think it should. In everything, we can and should give thanks and praise the Lord (I Thessalonians 5:18).

There is an erroneous assumption that because we did not feel or see a change or shift, that nothing happened. In spiritual and emotional realms, actual change may be more concealed (Proverbs 25:2). With regard to healing, God may choose to heal miraculously and reveal His power, He may heal over time which requires perseverance in prayer, and there are occasions where His answer is, "No." Even in the context of miraculous healing, 100% improvement may not be present after the initial prayer or issuing of commands (Mark 8:24-25). If there has been improvement, pray and command again.

If you feel stuck during a time of deliverance, it is wise to ask God to reveal if there is any element of unforgiveness that is preventing forward momentum. God may bring to mind a seemingly insignificant memory or one that was buried due to its intensity. He may use a word of knowledge to the worker in the form of a "word drop" or physical sensation somewhere in the body. If that happens, simply ask, "Does the fact that I heard or felt (fill in the blank) mean anything to you?" That should open the door to any forgiveness work needed before proceeding into other areas of deliverance.

We are representatives of the King of kings, and as such, we carry His authority and power. While we will be stern when addressing the evil spirits, shouting is not required. Jesus spoke; and therefore, we are also to speak remembering to do so in the authority given by the Name of Jesus.

Don't get a big head as a spiritual warrior. We are merely tools in the hand of a mighty God. "Not by might, nor by power, but by my Spirit, says the Lord of Hosts (Zechariah 4:6)." Our humility is of greater importance than our ability.

Our obedience is of utmost importance in every battle. "The horse is made ready for the day of battle, but the victory belongs to the Lord (Proverbs 21:31)."

At the end of a ministry session in which spiritual warfare is present, there are some important things that need to be done. You should seal any areas that spirits were kicked out of and fill them with the Holy Spirit. If you feel the session did not address all the unclean spirits, ask God to hold it and seal it until you can meet again. This does two things: first, it prevents the enemy from seeing the remaining vulnerabilities and sending reinforcements to that stronghold, and secondly, it permits the individual to experience the Fruit of the Spirit and realize the change in the places work was completed.

For the workers, those physically administering deliverance, as well as those supporting in prayer, it is good to clean off any potential attachments or points vulnerable to retaliation. These include your personhood (health, emotions, relationship integrity), and anyone or anything in your sphere of influence, such as family, pets, friends, church, clients, home, car, businesses, etc. For us, this was learned the hard way. After forgetting to "dust off" by commanding and praying off any evil attachments, Dallas found herself suffering from an unpleasant multi-symptom illness. Others have reported being agitated with spouses and have linked it to forgetting this essential element of work. It's easy to forget, because you're rejoicing in the victories or dealing with the physical symptoms of fatigue. If unusual things happen shortly after deliverance work, quickly review to see if you inadvertently missed this step.

When an individual experiences new freedoms through spiritual warfare, there are often other needs that must be addressed in their life. Generally, old habits will remain which require support and encouragement to break. If this is out of your scope of expertise, please help the person find a qualified Christian professional. There may be non-spiritual issues that need to be addressed by a doctor or mental health professional. Additionally, prior connections or ties with specific people or groups may need to be broken. This is not easy, as it is a big part of life and routine. Each one needs to create connections with new, healthier people and groups. Recognize what portion is yours to help them with and what portion will require others to assist. Helping them transition is more than just expecting them to attend a church service once a week.

We are all on a journey of growing in Christ. We need to be sure that, as we battle on behalf of others for freedom from the bondages of the enemy, we are also building them up in Christ. Jesus commanded us to "make disciples" (Matthew 28:19). To make disciples is not just to make converts, we need to be training, encouraging, guiding, and helping each other grow to be more and more Christ-like.

Finally, always give great thanks and praise to the Lord, for it is only with His direction, power, and authority, we are able to experience victory. Spend time actively confessing His Lordship, listening to praise and worship music, singing or playing an instrument, dancing in celebration and worship, waving a flag, painting, or whatever method of worship you enjoy. It is He alone that prepares you for battle, sustains you during the battle, and leads you to the banqueting table. Fight the good fight and celebrate His victories.

CHAPTER QUESTIONS

* How has God prepared you for battle?

* How is God sustaining you to continue in the battle?

* Describe an experience of victory and the Lord's banqueting table.

APPENDIX

LETTER ABOUT COMMANDING

This letter is an example of a way to command, provided as a guide to learn some of the things that we have found to be helpful in the process. There are no magic formulas for how to command the spirits to be bound and depart. We must follow the direction of the Holy Spirit in all aspects of deliverance including the commands given to the enemy.

Here are some things you need to keep in mind when commanding evil spirits:

1 John 4:4 and Ephesians 6:10-20

Ask God to fasten each piece on you.

Sometimes you can visualize this and sometimes you can't. Mine's purple.

The armor is metaphorical in the physical and actual in the spirit realm.

As you take the authority granted through Christ's death and resurrection, you need to be specific.

Address them by name (some emotions and spirits are known by the same name) if you know it. If the name is unknown, say, "All spirits impacting or assigned to ____, named, un-named, and known by any other names." (They use AKA's to dodge compliance.)

You don't want to allow them to further disrupt, so you should limit them, e.g., "I command you to stand at attention and freeze. You are not permitted to communicate with each other or any other dark spirits to gain strength. I bind you with the blood of Christ and command that you leave immediately taking no detour. You may not enter any other person, animal, living thing, geographical space, or inanimate object. You must go immediately to ____."

If you feel it necessary to unfreeze them, you can. We've not found that to be needed, because the commands are sequential with the last being for them to, "GO!"

You can instruct them to go to:
- The foot of the cross, but if you like to see yourself here when you pray, this is not a desirable choice
- To the Lake of Fire; this is temporary because God has given Satan limited power for a time
- To the feet of Jesus to acknowledge Him as King of Kings and Lord of Lords and have Him direct them afterward
- Dry places

Call their "bluff" or address technicalities just as you would with your children or students. The Holy Spirit will help you know what/how/when.

Commanding should be done aloud. Volume can vary from experience to experience and person to person.

We presume this goes without saying, but you need to keep prayed up and cleaned up in heart matters to exercise your authority well. If you want to read on this further, we suggest Charles Kraft's books, *I Give You Authority* and *Defeating Dark Angels*.

This is war, and you are on the winning side. Stand up even though you are wounded, and God will honor your obedience.

Romans 8:37, Psalm 116:1-19

WHY FLAGS?

"Why flags?" Because there is Scriptural basis, complimented by abundant symbolism in color and movement, and because worship is part of our spiritual warfare arsenal.

Synonyms for flags include banner, sign, signal, standard, standard-bearer, and symbol. While flags as we know them today are not mentioned specifically in Scripture, the present-day versions are adapted from the standards that were raised over each camp.

The people of Israel shall pitch their tents by their companies, each man in his own camp and each man by his own standard (Numbers 1:52). Current day flag waving can also be considered a precursor to the Saints waving palm branches around the Throne in Glory (Revelation 7:9-10).

The use of flags invites others to engage in worship in a different way than lifting hands, singing, or dancing, because it is a colorful visual representation of what is occurring in the spiritual realm. Flags can be used as an offering to God, to change the atmosphere, to decree a thing, to replace the spirit of heaviness, to lead into battle, for protection, and they can be used in the ministries of edification, healing, and restoration.

> I appeal to you therefore, brothers, by the mercies of God, to present your bodies as a living sacrifice, holy and acceptable to God, which is your spiritual worship. Do not be conformed to this world, but be transformed by the renewal of your mind, that by testing you may discern what is the will of God, what is good and acceptable and perfect (Romans 12:1-2).

As we offer our bodies as a living sacrifice, there are various ways this can be done. Some see this as walking in obedience through differing physical and spiritual disciplines; while others view this concept more through a lens of a physical expression of praise and worship, e.g., singing, playing a musical instrument, dance, art, flagging, etc. Flags are similar to instruments in that they are used as worship tools. As such, one can infer that flags are to lead in worship and spiritual warfare just as musicians do (2 Chronicles 5:12-14, Psalm 68:25). As flags are waved in God's presence, it is desired that the act be not only a testimony to those around, but even more so, it be received as a fragrant offering to our Lord (2 Corinthians 2:15-16a).

And all the Levitical singers, Asaph, Heman, and Jeduthun, their sons and kinsmen, arrayed in fine linen, with cymbals, harps, and lyres, stood east of the altar with 120 priests who were trumpeters; and it was the duty of the trumpeters and singers to make themselves heard in unison in praise and thanksgiving to the Lord), and when the song was raised, with trumpets and cymbals and other musical instruments, in praise to the Lord,

> "For He is good,
> for His steadfast love endures forever,"

the house, the house of the Lord, was filled with a cloud, so that the priests could not stand to minister because of the cloud, for the glory of the Lord filled the house of God (2 Chronicles 5:12-14).

The singers in front, the musicians last, between them virgins playing tambourines (Psalm 68:25).

For we are the aroma of Christ to God among those who are being saved and among those who are perishing, to one a fragrance from death to death, to the other a fragrance from life to life (2 Corinthians 2:15-16a).

Within the framework of personal worship, there is a natural outflow that will impact our surroundings. The use of flags can change the atmosphere; a shift in the spiritual realm that can be sensed but is beyond the experience or limitations of the physical realm. The flowing of the panels in a flag can also be considered a pictorial reminder of the outpouring of the Holy Spirit, as the sound of a mighty wind at the time of Pentecost (Acts 2:2).

> And suddenly there came from heaven a sound like a mighty rushing wind, and it filled the entire house where they were sitting (Acts 2:2).

On two separate occasions, Dallas has heard reports of intercessors experiencing visions related to specific locations and flags that she previously waved in each place. On one occasion, Dallas had gone early to wave a Lion of Judah flag throughout the Sanctuary/Worship Center prior to others arriving. A report of someone seeing a vision of Jesus walking through and touching people during the service followed. Weeks later, she waved a flag that has a gold panel and a rainbow panel which is named His Presence/Shekhinah on the platform near the drums. Again, this was done as an act of preparation without any fanfare or public awareness. Later, the report came back that someone had seen a vision of Jesus standing there with rainbow colors all around saying, "Yes, I am here." Dallas received these reports as God validating what she was doing in private through the use of flags to prepare an atmosphere for others to encounter the Living God.

Like all other instruments of worship, it is not the flag creating the change, rather it is partnering with what God is already doing through the Holy Spirit. In such a context, flags can also be used to decree a thing within God's will and tear down strongholds (2 Corinthians 10:3-4, Matthew 18:18-20).

> For though we walk in the flesh, we are not waging war according to the flesh. For the weapons of our warfare are not of the flesh but have divine power to destroy strongholds (2 Corinthians 10:3-4).

> Truly, I say to you, whatever you bind on earth shall be bound in heaven, and whatever you loose on earth shall be loosed in heaven. Again I say to you, if two of you agree on earth about anything they ask, it will be done for them by my Father in heaven. For where two or three are gathered in my name, there am I among them. (Matthew 18:18-20)

Waving a flag can result in a personal shift from being burdened by a spirit of heaviness to entering into His courts with praise. The fabric of the flag in this instance becomes a physical reminder of the garment of praise in Isaiah 61:3.

> to grant to those who mourn in Zion—
>   to give them a beautiful headdress instead of ashes,

> the oil of gladness instead of mourning,
> the garment of praise instead of a faint spirit;
> that they may be called oaks of righteousness,
> the planting of the Lord, that he may be glorified
> Isaiah 61:3.

Dallas has had so many say to her that they were glad they came to flag practice, because it renewed their spirit after a difficult day or week.

When comparing current day flags to tribe standards or banners, we must consider their use in battle. The Lord Himself is our Banner (Exodus 17:15), and He trains our hands for war and our fingers for battle (Psalm 18:34, Psalm 144:1). While we do not war against flesh and blood (Ephesians 6:12) and while the battle is the Lord's (2 Chronicles 20:15, 1 Samuel 17:47), we partner with Him in obedience and put our faith into action.

When He directed armies of the Old Testament into battle, there were protocols to be followed (see Numbers 4, Numbers 10, and Deuteronomy 20). The banners led the procession to announce the tribe or camp. It is interesting to note that not only were the Israelites instructed to encircle those that they were overtaking (Deuteronomy 20:12, Joshua 5:13-6:2), but God also instructed that the Levites would camp *around* the tabernacle to *protect* the people from God's wrath (Numbers 1:51-53).

Flags can also be used to encourage the Body of Christ and non-believers alike when they are used to minister in acts of physical healing. While healing can occur spiritually and emotionally, the physical is an observable manifestation of the power of God who is our Healer.

> Bless the Lord, O my soul,
> and forget not all his benefits,
> who forgives all your iniquity,
> who heals all your diseases (Psalms 103:2-3).

If you have been asking God for renewal, revival, or a deepened worship experience whether privately or corporately as a church body, flags may be a way He is trying to usher in more of His Presence. If you serve in a leadership capacity, we would encourage you to consider how to incorporate and establish this powerful tool and instrument as part of your overall worship ministry.

Originally posted at www.lydiadabar.com by Dallas Henslee

QUESTIONS AND ANSWERS

What is the difference between demon possession and demonic influence?

While it may seem like semantics, we believe there is a difference between demon possession and demonic influence. Possession indicates ownership, while influence allows an effect on the person but not ownership. We do *not* believe that Christians can be possessed (owned) by a demon though non-believers can.

Think about an infection in the body. The infection has been given an entrance such as through a cut. Once in the body, it may be able to multiply and effect the person, thereby influencing how they feel and act. While the infection has influence on the body, it does not own the person. Similarly, a demon may have been given a way into a person's body or soul (thoughts and emotions) and have the ability to influence them, but it cannot own a believer's spirit, as that has been given to the Lord and indwelt by the Holy Spirit.

We believe that demonic influence is possible for all people. When we are counseling with Christians that have demonic influence, sometimes we will use the phrase "kick them out" when what we are doing is cutting off their influence from the person's life.

Demonic influence can come about through a variety of choices that a believer makes. These include, but are not limited to, unrepented sins, vows, participation in occult activity, and abuse. These activities which allow demonic influence may take place before or after salvation.

Will a habitual sin lead to a demon?

A habitual sin is an unrepented sin. We are commanded to repent of our sins; not just confess them (Proverbs 28:13). Repentance includes confessing or admitting to the sin but also requires turning away from it and turning towards God (Acts 3:19). There is a change in what is being done as John the Baptist describes in Luke 3:10-14. In other words, to repent of a sin is to stop doing it and start doing what is right before the Lord. Therefore, if we are habitually participating in the same sin, we have not repented, but merely expressed remorse.

We do not believe that a habitual sin will always lead to demonic influence. It does, however, give the enemy an area of our life that is open for attack and exploitation. If we allow the sin to continue, and the enemy exploits that area of our life, then he is able to dwell there. We call these strongholds, which can develop through unrepented sin as well as through agreements and vows. It is a place that we have allowed the enemy to occupy because of our choices. For a harsher look at making a practice of sin look at 1 John 3:8-9.

Since we are new creatures when we are saved, doesn't salvation free us of all demonic attachments?

Salvation secures our spirit. There will often be a newness of life in our body and soul at the time of salvation but that is not guaranteed. Nor does it mean that we are instantly free of all the past attachments and influences that we have allowed in our life. For example, someone may be a member of a gang when they come to know Christ as their Savior. While they may leave the gang, it will not be without effort and difficulty.

We must work out our salvation (Philippians 2:12) by renewing our mind and putting on the mind of Christ (Romans 12:2, Ephesians 4:17-24). If salvation was the end all, then we wouldn't have these other instructions. For example Paul tells the Philippian church that even he has not obtained perfection but to press on toward the goal (Philippians 3:12-16).

The Bible seems to be silent, or very quiet, about exorcising demons out of believers. Shouldn't it give us a pattern of treatment that would clearly address its application for believers?

There is quite a bit of discussion in Scripture about demons and deliverance. What is generally not clear in Scripture is its application to believers versus non-believers. However, we must not ignore what is said in favor of that which is not.

Who did Jesus cast demons out of? It was people that came to Him and called Him "Lord." He taught in the synagogues and cast out demons (Mark 1:39). We can separate these actions but it is best to keep them together as stated in Scripture. He taught in the synagogue to call people to believe in Him as the Son of God. He cast out demons, in or very near to the synagogue. The people who came to Him, came in belief. Notice that He did not cast demons out of the Pharisees as they did not believe in Him.

Isaiah prophesied about Christ in Isaiah 53. What Christ did is available to all people, but only those who believe will receive the promises. In Matthew 8:16-17, Jesus casts out the spirits of those "who were oppressed by demons" in fulfillment of Isaiah 53:4-5. The promises of Isaiah are for those who acknowledge Christ as Lord, so it is a reasonable conclusion that Jesus was delivering believers in Matthew 8.

There are other practices in the Church that are not given large volumes of specifics in Scripture. For example, two ordinances of the Church are Baptism and Communion. While these are accepted and practiced ordinances, there really isn't a lot of detail provided in the Bible about them. Jesus instructed His disciples to baptize in the name of the Father, the Son, and the Holy Spirit (Matthew 28:19-20). There are examples of baptism occurring in rivers, pools, and other bodies of water, but no clear direction on the actual procedures to be followed.

With communion, the various branches and denominations of the Church don't even agree on what to call it, whether Communion, Eucharist, the Lord's Supper, or the Bread and the Cup. In the Gospels, we are told about Jesus breaking the bread and passing it to the disciples followed by the cup (Matthew 26:26-28, Mark 14:22-24, and Luke 17:17-20). In 1 Corinthians 11:23-29, Paul gives us instructions about our attitude and taking the elements in a worthy manner. But there are not clear instructions on what type of juice or wine to use, the exact type of bread, the frequency, whether to walk to the front or pass the elements out, or whether to take together or individually.

Since there are so few instructions given on baptism and communion, should we then assume that Christians are not to follow these ordinances regularly? We don't believe so. The same can be applied about our interaction with the spirit realm (angelic and demonic).

Just as cultural understanding gives us insight to baptism and communion, it also influences our understanding of spirits. Even today, there are places in the world that culturally recognize spirits and their influence on humans more than other places. The western cultures of the twenty first century generally do not give much credence to spirits except in entertainment. This cultural lens has influenced how the western church approaches dealing with spirits.

Who are we permitted to work with for deliverance?

We recommend that a determination of the person's relationship with Christ is important prior to any deliverance work. If the individual is unable to say "Jesus is Lord," then we will generally not proceed in casting out any spirits. There may be a need to bind a spirit that is controlling the person's ability to make a decision of their own will to accept Christ's offer of salvation.

Without the protection of the individual's spirit by the indwelling of the Holy Spirit through faith in Jesus Christ as

Lord and Savior, there is a potential for any work that we do to be undone leaving the person in a worse condition in the end (Luke 11:24-26 and Matthew 12:43-45). Therefore, as a general rule, we do not practice deliverance work with non-believers. We do, however, share with them about Christ's love and sacrifice.

How do you get permission from the person needing deliverance?

Since each person has free-will and is able to exercise authority over their life, it is important to have their permission before proceeding in deliverance. Generally, we will ask if they want to be free from the influence of the demonic. They need to make the conscious decision to seek freedom, not have us coerce them into it.

In addition to obtaining an individual's consent to enter deliverance and inner healing work, we need to be aware of any authority structures and issues arising from such. These may arise because a person in authority over the individual is not in agreement with the process of deliverance. In some cases, the individual may want to proceed while the one in authority over them does not. First, pray that God would make a way to be able to continue. Second, do not pressure or manipulate. If the one in authority persists in prohibiting deliverance work, pray that God will continue to work with the willing individual as they pray, read, and listen to biblical teaching. You may have been the seed that another will water and yet another will harvest.

There are times when we should bind a spirit regardless of the person's permission like when Paul cast the spirit out of the slave girl in Acts 16:16-18. When permission is not obtained from the person, there may be undesirable consequences such as Paul and Silas being beaten and jailed. Ultimately, we are responsible to be obedient to the Holy Spirit, not to man. Therefore, we should proceed with much prayer and submission to the Lord.

I'm just a lay person with no special training. How can I be effective in spiritual warfare?

We believe that ALL believers are called to battle in the spirit realm and are so equipped (Ephesians 6:10-18). A "professional" may have more knowledge and understanding but does not have any more power or authority in the spirit realm.

There are times that it is helpful to understand the hierarchy, functions, and names of spirits but it is not always necessary. Since all deliverance is only possible through the authority and power of God (Father, Son and Holy Spirit), we are no more or less powerful in deliverance than any other believer.

I'm unsure about the right words to say. How do I know that I'm doing it correctly?

While the occult generally has special words and phrases that must be said in a certain order, we don't find that formulas are of great importance. When battling, we must be in communion with the Holy Spirit and dependent upon Him for the words to be spoken.

When first encountering spiritual warfare or deliverance ministry, it can be helpful to follow in the footsteps of those who have gone before us. Therefore, we have shared our experiences and samples of ways in which to address spirits. The examples given in the book are just that, examples. The more you walk with the Holy Spirit in deliverance ministry, the easier it will be to know what to say in each situation.

Methods vary, interpretations are different, but it is the Lord who is all powerful and able to deliver. He desires our obedience over any sacrifice that we could offer (1 Samuel 15:22, Matthew 12:6-7). That means that our methods are of lesser importance than our obedience. We are responsible for our obedience to the Lord's directions.

What if I do it wrong, will the person be worse off?

Jesus speaking about a spirit being cast out and then returning with seven more spirits and making the individual worse off (Luke 11:24-26 and Matthew 12:43-45), has been used as an argument against deliverance ministries. The fear is that if everything isn't done just perfectly, the person will end up with even more spirits. This is a very real possibility for an unbeliever whose spirit is not inhabited by the Holy Spirit. However, Christians are protected in our innermost being (our spirits).

When we are operating in the power of Christ and with the guidance of the Holy Spirit, even if we don't do everything just right, He is more than able to overcome our failings. We have found that even when we make mistakes, the Lord is gracious and protects the individual. Also remember that we are cutting off the demonic influence, so even if there are pieces left, the individual won't be worse than beforehand.

We also close each session in prayer, specifically asking the Holy Spirit to fill any spaces left empty. Sealing off the area with the blood of Christ provides an extra covering of protection.

What if the spirits don't depart?

We are ultimately not responsible for the outcome. Our primary focus needs to be obedience to the Lord (The greatest commandment Matthew 22:37). Our secondary focus needs to be to love the people we are encountering (Matthew 22:39). The rest is up to the Lord to bring to fruition through our obedient actions.

There may be a number of reasons that a spirit doesn't depart when commanded. The individual may still be holding onto something that is giving the spirit a right to stay such as unforgiveness. There may be a secondary curse that needs to be broken. We may be dealing with something other than a spirit. Mental and emotional issues are complex and can be caused by a multitude of things including spirits, physical injury, hormonal imbalance, chemicals, etc. If we think that all problems are caused by an evil spirit then we are likely to miss helping those with non-spiritual issues.

What role do prayer and fasting have in deliverance?

Prayer is vital as we must be in communication with the Father throughout the process. We are not operating in our own knowledge and strength, therefore we must be receiving instructions and that requires prayer. Prayer is not just talking to God, or requesting His intervention; prayer is having a conversation with the Lord. We invite Him into the session as if He were physically in the room.

Fasting is sometimes needed for victory. Jesus said in Matthew 17:21, "But this kind does not go out except by prayer and fasting" (NASB). Fasting is an act of submission to the Lord and therefore weakens the demons. We have found that when the individual seeking deliverance fasts prior to a session the work is generally easier, and more can be accomplished in less time.

Some of the people who are doing deliverance appear to be charlatans or frauds. How can we be sure that we are not being deceived?

Yes, there are plenty of charlatans and frauds. That is true of every aspect of religion and church movements. We must always be watchful for false teachers and test what is being taught by comparing it to Scripture (in its entirety, not proof texting) as taught by Paul, throughout his letters, and Peter (2 Peter 2). Just because the most visible and vocal on a given subject are not presenting the truth, or are in it for the money, doesn't mean that everyone in that arena is a false teacher.

To only use one teacher's source is limited at best and highly dangerous at worst. This is one of the reasons we place a disclaimer regarding the sources we quote. While we may agree with the statement provided, we reserve the right to disagree with other tenets of their teachings. There are many who have written on spiritual warfare. Seek a breadth of teachings from a variety of backgrounds and generations, and always compare to Scripture. By reading multiple perspectives, including those that you may disagree with, and taking it to Scripture and prayer, you are able to develop a more comprehensive understanding of the spirit realm and deliverance ministry.

Is our interacting with demons just a distraction from what we should be doing?

Distraction is a method that the enemy uses against believers. Look around the western church and you will see a very large contingency of busy people. Busyness is one of the best distractions he can employ. He will also use differing theological positions to get us to argue with each other about the correct interpretation or application of Scripture.

Another distraction is to tie us up in battle unnecessarily. This can be through various means including things like interacting with the spirits, asking questions, feeling the need to know everything before casting them out, etc. We have found that the more we operate in deliverance the more efficient the process seems to be. There are things that we need to know, but we get this information from the individual or from the Holy Spirit, not the enemy. Avoid drawing out the process as much as possible.

There are safeguards that can be implemented in deliverance sessions. It is good to have multiple workers and prayer covering as well as allotting a reasonable amount of time to work together. Too little time and you will feel rushed and possibly anxious. Too much time and everyone may succumb to fatigue. We find it helpful to place limitations on the demons such as not allowing them to speak or communicate with other spirits. We also disallow them to physically harm the client or others present. Additionally, we prohibit them from finding another host nearby. We often phrase that as not permitting them to detour or attach to other people, living things, geographic spaces, or inanimate objects. Jewelry, souvenirs from foreign lands, items used in religious rituals, etc. are examples of objects that might be favored by demons.

We also do not believe that allowing the spirit to manifest is good practice in most cases. If they try to manifest, we will limit them to prevent physical or additional emotional harm. There are times when some manifestation is beneficial such as if the person needs a physical confirmation of the spirit and its departure or when in a culture that is accustomed to physical manifestation and needs to see it to acknowledge the deliverance.

Is it true that if I don't give demons any credence, then they are unable to attack me?

Another of the schemes of the enemy is to get us to think little of them and thereby get us to ignore or not fight them. For a good analogy about this scheme, read *The Screwtape Letters* by C.S. Lewis.

We are very aware of their power and potential to influence. God has allowed them a certain level of influence on the earth for a time. They are limited, but they also have great ability to harm and inflict pain, even in believers.

Simply not acknowledging them or their abilities does not mean they aren't able to attack. If we think by not locking our doors and believing that God will protect our stuff no robber will be able to come in and steal, we are setting ourselves up for potential loss. Just as robbers are real and don't follow the law, demons are real and don't fight fairly.

Is it enough to build up our spiritual armor and make a defensive stand to resist the devil?

We are absolutely to put on our armor and resist the devil (Ephesians 6:11, James 4:7, 1 Peter 5:8-9). We are also to not wage war according to the flesh (2 Corinthians 10:3-6). We are to use our offensive weapons which include the Word of God (Hebrews 4:12) and prayer. The Blood of Christ is also a powerful offensive and defensive weapon.

The pieces of the armor that are often considered defensive can also be used offensively. For example Truth and Faith are incredibly powerful weapons to be used to defeat the lies and attacks of the enemy. When we live our lives in Truth we not only don't give the enemy an opportunity to attack, we also are able to bring to light his lies and schemes around us. He would rather not have any of his activities in the light.

Other weapons we have available to us include the gifts of the Holy Spirit (1 Corinthians 12) which includes words of knowledge and discernment. We do not ask the enemy to give us information as he is a liar, so what he says is suspect. We depend on the Holy Spirit to provide words of knowledge. We also rely heavily on the Holy Spirit's discernment when determining what is to be addressed and how.

If we were to be passive, then we don't think the Lord would have given so many instructions in Scripture to battle. Jesus was not passive when it came to healing people and casting out demons. Nor were the apostles and other followers of Christ in the first century church. We are instructed to share the Gospel and bring freedom to the captives (Isaiah 61:1, Galatians 5:1, most of the book of Romans).

God gave permission for Satan to sift Job. It seems I should simply plead with him in prayer to bring deliverance. If God is allowing it, how can I fight against a particular circumstance?

There are times when difficulties come into our life and we have the choice of how to respond. Does God cause these things? Some might unequivocally say, "No." However, we think sometimes He causes them to bring about His character in our life or for an intended impact. Obviously, if it has occurred, then at minimum He has allowed it to happen. Does that mean we are to just accept it and dwell there? We don't think that is the only allowable response.

Scripture tells us that we are to grow in the midst of difficulties (James 1:2-4, Romans 5:1-5). If we simply suffer through, the rate of growth is reduced which will extend the time of difficulty.

There are times that we face hard things in life that God desires for us to confront and obtain victory. We are more than conquerors through Christ (Romans 8:37). There are multiple examples in Scripture where God said to fight. Just a few are:

- Israelites instructed to take possession of the Promised Land (Joshua 1:2-9)
- David told to defeat various enemies (1 Samuel 23:2, 30:8, 2 Samuel 5:17-19)
- We are to take up our armor and battle (Ephesians 6:10-18)
- We are to fight the good fight (1 Timothy 1:18 and 6:12)

Some may think that Job just accepted the circumstances and went on with his life. There are 42 long, hard chapters in the Book of Job. He wrestled with God through the process, yet he never cursed God. In the end, he realized that he was nothing, and God was everything. Job's test is likely different than your test which is different than ours. God will have different purposes for the tests that we face in life.

In all situations, we must go to the Father to determine what it is that we are to be doing in response. Our experience is that He rarely tells us to just sit there and endure it. There always seems to be a lesson or growth process in the hard parts of life, and to find those, we have to engage with the Lord in the circumstance.

Some Christians seem to think demons have more influence and control than they do. How do you approach intimidation and fear?

Fear is one of the tools that the enemy uses to bind people - both unbelievers and believers. Fear is not of God (2 Timothy 1:7, 1 John 4:18, Psalm 34:4). We do not fear the demons. When we are in right standing before the Father, we have nothing to fear. However, when we are living in sin, we are choosing to allow opportunities for the enemy (Ephesians 4:27).

The demons do have significant influence and control in this world. It is important to remember that greater is He that is in me than he that is in the world (1 John 4:4). Through the power of Christ's Blood we are able to stand righteous before the throne of God and before the enemy.

I've had some success and others are telling me that I'm powerful in deliverance ministry. How should I respond to these compliments?

It is nice to hear compliments and praise from people that are experiencing freedom and those who know them. Be exceedingly careful to receive these statements with humility. Pride is very dangerous and can cause us to fall (Proverbs 16:18). If we start to operate in pride, we are allowing the enemy an opportunity to attack and potentially knock out our ministry and those around us.

All of our power and authority comes through Christ. We must not allow our ego to be built up through the praise of others or the success of our ministry. In no way are we to take from or even share God's glory (Isaiah 42:8, 48:11). Receive compliments with humility and be sure to give God all of the glory.

IN DEFENSE OF A WARFARE WORLDVIEW

We are aware that not everyone agrees with our approach to spiritual warfare. In acknowledgement of that fact, we have attempted to share how we approach our position Biblically. In the summer of 2018, we were sent an article that shared an opposing viewpoint. The following is our response.

Immediately upon reading the provided account, I wrote a margin note that says, "God doesn't share His glory." (Isaiah 42:8, 48:11) It presents a recollection of a woman saying Satan was afraid of a particular individual, when in actuality, Satan only feared the authority given because of the shed blood of Christ and a personal relationship with Jesus. More to the point, Satan fears, and must submit to, Jesus Christ and the Triune, Living God alone.

The writer indicates that within a Warfare Worldview the outcome of the battle is uncertain, removing the Sovereign nature of God's character. While we embrace and teach a

Warfare Worldview, we do not agree with this assertion. Rather, we believe that God already knows the outcome. He sealed it when Jesus died on the cross as The Perfect Sacrifice for the sin of all mankind; therefore, we fight from a position of victory obtained by Christ in His resurrection. The battle is the Lord's (2 Chronicles 20:15, Zechariah 4:6, 1 Samuel 17:47), we simply partner with Him during our time on earth.

In a quest to prove oneself a mighty warrior, it is possible to labor at all hours doing deliverance work; seeing some individuals briefly, and others constantly over several years. The focus of such a schedule seems to be on the work of man hoping to achieve a certain level of reputation. We teach that this is a tactic employed by Satan (Lucifer, the Devil, the enemy). If he cannot get you to stop through intimidation, he will attempt to keep you so busy that you burn out whether physically, mentally, emotionally, spiritually, or any combination of those. It is easy to fall into the trap of being so desperately needed, that one fails to maintain appropriate self-care boundaries. The lure, of course, is that you are doing much needed work in the Kingdom of God. This is dangerous ground, as it borders on pride, and once one is ensnared by pride, there is only one result, i.e. a destructive fall (Proverbs 16:18).

In the commentary, Bob Larson is quoted in a way that the reader presumes Larson is THE authority on deliverance. It is apparent from the citations, that the commentator largely develops his argument against a Warfare Worldview based on Larson's beliefs.

It is our position that following a single teacher is often dangerous, because you inherit their bias. It is healthier to consult multiple sources, taking each to Scripture and holding onto only that which stands in alignment with the Truth. We have found that it is easy to misquote or misinterpret a source that holds beliefs contrary to one's own. We have also experienced a progression of learning and engaging in spiritual warfare as the Lord has continued to train us, meaning simply that our methods have changed over time, but God's Truth has not.

Again, the sole authority on deliverance is Christ, our Deliverer, Savior, Redeemer, Great Physician, and Wonderful Counselor. In full disclosure, we have not read Larson's book as referenced in the article. We have, however, read other materials of his. While we see value in portions of what Larson teaches, we do not agree with his position completely. One of the places we differ is in the necessity to use exact wording to break off demonic influence. If you agree that God knows all (in other words, is omniscient), then it follows that the Holy Spirit is aware of how the unholy influence came about and can direct how it is to be broken. Because Christ's blood covers all believers, we do not need to use the methods that Satan employs by engaging specific words in a prescribed order, such as those used in magic, spells, hexes, etc. We hold to

The Truth and The Word, and The Lord cancels out the consequences as He chooses. To spend excessive time attempting to determine who, what, when, where, why, and exact uttered phrases when referring to the demonic is a waste of time and energy. Never mind that it gives the enemy exceedingly more air time and glory than he deserves.

In response to concepts this individual references as having previously taught, specifically, the legal rights of demons, we teach something similar. There is the possibility that the entities will not remove themselves until the deliverance worker(s), and possibly the believer being delivered, spend time fasting and praying (Mark 9:29). In our experience, demons that have been cast out will challenge the victory by making it *appear* they never really left. This is simply a shift from internal influence in one's soul to an external attempt to influence. They are simply employing a battlefield tactic of trying to retake the ground they just lost. They are verifying that the area they were cast from has been secured by the Holy Spirit.

Noticeably missing in the section in which the writer explains how people were taught to continue to experience freedom, is faith, forgiveness, and salvation. Jesus often said it was a person's faith that had made them well. This omission could account for the need for numerous repeat deliverance sessions, as could the fact that deliverance counselors usually do not engage in any part of psychological care to avoid overstepping their understanding and credentials. Trauma can create spiritual bondage, but the trauma work itself unfortunately may be neglected in this approach due to lack of knowledge on the part of the minister.

The discourse is continued by looking at Secret Spiritual Laws. There is an apparent connotation that anything secret is not of God. Later in the commentary, the author firmly states that all secrets are of the occult, and yet Scripture tells us that God has purposed to keep some things hidden or secret (Deuteronomy 29:29, Jeremiah 33:3, Daniel 2:22, Proverbs 25:2, Isaiah 45:3). While secrecy is often an indication that one should more closely investigate the potential of occult involvement, it is quite possible that what is now considered secret are Biblical principles that the church discontinued teaching and are; therefore, unknown by the general populace. It is a burdensome position to presume that one must understand everything about a concept for it to be true. Again, God designed that not everything about Him is discoverable.

Another spiritual law that is purported to be a part of Warfare Worldview is that "demons are able to move in when a person has a passive will." We do not agree that passivity in and of itself should be considered the basis for demonic intrusion; while believing that passivity following another action could permit the unholy spirit(s) to remain.

This occurs because they are not being commanded to leave. Shame resulting in an unwillingness to admit something that has occurred in the past or exercised passivity could also be the result of an unrepentant heart. Being sorry that you got caught or having to live with unpleasant consequences is not the same as wanting to rout out, turn from, or eradicate a behavior contrary to God's holy nature. In this case, passivity has a rebellious quality accompanying it. There is a need for confession, repentance, and requesting God's forgiveness.

In reading the statement that passive people did not display a strong will, one ought to consider whether or not this was more accurately a display of hopelessness and depression. Both these states compromise a person's ability to engage in life well, much less spiritual warfare and deliverance. While some unclean spirits are known by the same names as emotions, unpleasant emotions do not always indicate a demonic presence. This is a place in which inner healing and deliverance collide and therefore, they must be addressed concurrently.

None of what is accomplished in God's Kingdom is based solely on human effort. This includes but is not limited to willing ourselves to be stronger or engaging in deliverance ministry. Jeremiah 17:5, 7 is quoted as an argument against such ministries; however, we see that this verse actually celebrates God's authority while diminishing the wisdom and power of man in his own right. Contrary to the originally stated position, this verse supports deliverance ministries which depend on God for everything.

Who determines the outcome; is it God or humans and demons? God does. Free will exists, and it is possible that an individual may miss out on the blessing God intended for them due to delay or disobedience. In such a case, God will bring about His ultimate will through another that is willing to submit to His always perfect direction.

There is a driving force behind much of the presentation against adopting a Warfare Worldview that depends on the human element asserting that in this view, the battle is between humans and unholy or wicked spirits. Given that statement alone, were it true, we would abandon this worldview as it would be contradicted by Scripture. Rather, we hold that the battle is the Lord's and we partner with Him much like the armies in the Old Testament. The only way we have authority to enter this spiritual battleground is under the covering of Christ; therefore, the battle is The Holy Spirit against unholy spirits with God leading the charge. God is all knowing, and therefore, the exorcist/deliverance counselor/minister need not feel the pressure of exacting the information from the tormenting spirit(s). Furthermore, while there is a hierarchy, it is not necessary to identify all its levels to stand against it. Demons lie, so we put our faith in God for the revelation of what needs to be done.

The revelation of the meaning of the Scriptures is through asking the Holy Spirit to speak to our spirit. We are constantly listening for the Lord's direction as we partner with Him to minister deliverance. There are times that we quote or read extended Scripture passages during deliverance and inner healing work. There are also times that God instructs us through Words of Knowledge and Discernment. A.W. Tozer seems to agree with the position that God speaks to His children through the Canon and post Canon.

> The Bible is the written word of God, and because it is written it is confined and limited by the necessities of ink and paper and leather. The Voice of God, however, is alive and free as the sovereign God is free. "The words that I speak unto you, they are spirit, and they are life." The life is in the speaking words. God's word in the Bible can have power only because it corresponds to God's word in the universe. It is the present Voice which makes the written Word all-powerful. Otherwise it would lie locked in slumber within the covers of a book. (Tozer, A.W., *The Pursuit of God,* pp 48-49)

We often work in teams because of the quantity and intensity of the material present in any given session. It is also common for us to take notes, so that we can stay on track or not skip anything that was mentioned. The volume and velocity of discovery are rapid. We do not use the notes as a way of recording statements of the demons. There is no need to record what they are saying if those wicked spirits have been commanded to be silent.

In his quest for truth, the article's author says his main concern is whether or not the Warfare Worldview can be defended Biblically. We believe such a worldview can be defended Biblically although not the way it is represented in his article. Jesus serves as our advocate, covering, and mediator before the Father (Revelation 12:10; Hebrews 9:15, 1 Timothy 2:5, 1 John 2:1). The demonic realm has already been defeated by Christ's death and resurrection. While this has already been accomplished, we are confined by time, and we live on the earth with demonic oppression until God calls an end to time. With this in mind, the view of the necessity of full discovery and exploitation of the demonic hierarchy goes against Scripture. We needn't discover something that God already told us exists, and exploitation would infer that we have something to gain. In as much as we perceive the gain as personal achievement, we dare to infringe upon God's glory.

The belief that we need "professional exorcists" falls completely in line with the culture of the Western church in which we have professional teachers and worshipers. This is a fallacy on all counts. We are a priesthood of believers, imitators of Christ. As such, we are all to bring freedom to captives; we are all to teach and disciple; and we are all to worship.

As demons are fallen angels, we believe that in the authority of Christ, we have the command from Christ to expel them (Matthew 10:8, Mark 16:17-18). We believe that God commissions believers to engage in battles against spirits of darkness and equips us for each battle. Be aware that it is extremely dangerous for a deliverance minister to operate in his own wisdom, picking and choosing which tools to use. This is actually still at God's discretion. If one has chosen to proceed in their own power, then it is accurate to place responsibility for the outcome on the deliverance worker. If the worker is simply a vessel available for the Lord to work through, it is possible to have the individual being helped address their personal will and emotions that are being negatively impacted.

In regards to the need to address a Gatekeeper spirit, we have not encountered such in our ministry. That isn't to say this teaching should be dismissed outright, but in our experience, we have found it adequate to command all team members, no matter their role, to depart. The Holy Spirit is more than able to mandate that all entities are arranged and accounted for completely. We also seal off the areas by the blood of Christ, so the demons are not permitted to return on their own.

There is substantial discussion in Scripture about demons and deliverance. What is generally not clear in Scripture is its application to believers versus non-believers. Much of this discrepancy arises from the progression of time. Jesus ministered for three years; healing the sick, casting out demons, and teaching His followers. It is our position, that each of these individuals Christ touched believed in Him, having their faith or belief counted as righteousness prior to His death, resurrection and the sending of the Holy Spirit, much like Abraham (Genesis 15:6).

To address the concern that the work done within the framework of a Warfare Worldview is solely post Biblical Canon, consider the following. Jesus cast demons out of people that came to Him and called Him "Lord." He taught in the synagogues and cast out demons (Mark 1:39). He cast out demons, in or very near the synagogue which served as a community gathering place, as well as a place of teaching. He cast seven demons out of Mary Magdalene (Mark 16:9) and delivered the Gadarenes demoniac (Mark 5:1-20) as well as others. The people who came to Him, came in belief. In contrast, He did not cast demons out of the Pharisees, as they were offended by Him and chose not to believe in Him. He commanded His disciples, both those present for the admonition and those to come, to do as He had modeled during His time on earth. To assert that we can only provide deliverance to non-believers, because true believers are filled with The Holy Spirit (Ephesians 4:20-24), seems to greatly diminish, if not completely discredit, the works of our Lord and Savior towards those He delivered and healed during His earthly ministry.

Isaiah prophesied about Christ in Isaiah 53. What Christ did is available to all people, but only those who believe will receive the promises. In Matthew 8:16-17, Jesus casts out the spirits of those "who were oppressed by demons" in fulfillment of Isaiah 53:4-5. The promises of Isaiah are for those who acknowledge Christ as Lord, so it is a reasonable conclusion that Jesus was delivering believers in Matthew 8.

There are other practices in the Church that are not given large volumes of specifics in Scripture. For example, two ordinances of the Church are Baptism and Communion. While these are accepted and practiced ordinances, there really is not a lot of detail provided in the Bible about them. Since there are so few instructions given on baptism and communion, should we then assume that Christians are not to follow these ordinances regularly? We don't believe that to be true. The same can be applied about our interaction with the spirit realm (angelic and demonic).

There is an erroneous presumption made that spiritual senses are not as valid as physical ones, and a mind that ponders spiritual matters is not sound or rational. Given that most Christians believe we are eternal spiritual beings clothed for a specified time in a temporal physical body, this argument seems limited at best.

To contend that God does not reveal the name of demons, places one in a position of being an authority on God. We take the position that He does not always share this information, but that He can if He chooses. Remember that God sent an angel to Daniel who shared that he had been detained by the Prince of Persia (Daniel 10:13). With this in mind, since God is unchangeable, is it too far a leap of faith to believe that He can still share with us in the context of a personal, intimate, spiritual relationship, names or circumstances which are impacting our personal lives?

We are uncomfortable with the approach that appears to allow us to exact revenge or place judgement on the enemy. This portion of the battle belongs to God alone (Deuteronomy 32:35, Proverbs 20:22, Romans 12:19, Hebrews 10:30). Additionally, while we have authority over fallen angels, we do not believe we currently have authority over those that have remained pure. Scripture says we were made a little lower than the angels (Psalms 8:5, Hebrews 2:7, 9); and therefore, we ask God to send the appropriate types and quantity for any situation we feel His messengers are needed.

The commentator states that it is necessary to engage with demons to learn the rules. We unequivocally disagree. God is the Creator of all that exists. Nothing takes Him by surprise. He knows all, sees all, and is everywhere. He still heals and performs miracles. He is the ultimate Victor, King of kings and Lord of lords which means He knows the rules of the spirit realm — all of them. We do not have to engage with the enemy in order to learn Satan's tactics. We do, however, need to remain in fellowship with God. The focus is not on the devourer, but rather it should always be on The Deliverer.

There are places where we agree with the Providential Worldview in addition to viewing life through the Warfare Worldview and do not see that the two seemingly opposed positions must necessarily exclude each other. For example, 2 Timothy 2:24-26, "People in bondage to Satan escape only when God grants repentance!" In other words, it is *NOT* dependent on the deliverance worker's desire, efforts, skill, or time.

People are drawn to Christians, because of God's love in which we are living and operating from daily. Many, ourselves included, would fail to see how some deliverance procedures primarily utilized in the past would display such kindness. Screaming at someone and physically restraining them, or going as far as to physically harm the body as demons manifest themselves, are not loving acts.

There is a way of working in deliverance ministry that is much gentler; while it is still being effective. Often, we will conclude a session having not had the need to even raise our voices. Our approach is to care for the individual to the best of our ability; while at the same time we are dealing with the unwanted demonic spirits. When appropriate, our sessions also incorporate teaching. Jesus said, "Go make disciples;" not just evangelize converts (Matthew 28:19). Discipleship is probably the most effective way we have found to deal with unhealthy behaviors, thoughts, and words.

We also have discovered that not only do those we work with have limits, but so do we. We put in boundaries and safeguards to lessen the fatigue and hold burnout at bay.

We commend individuals for striving to defend their Worldview from a Biblical standpoint; however, a preference to embrace extremes rather than evaluating previously believed half-truths is an incomplete process. The article's author said he was making the assumption that the Gospel was insufficient as a result of his interpretation of the circumstances. Within this statement, there is not a clear profession of faith from those with whom he worked.

He said those he worked with had met or encountered Christ. Actual salvation experiences in which these individuals repented, died to sin, and invited the Holy Spirit to come and reside inside them making Christ their Lord and a Savior was not mentioned. This is imperative! We desire that those we work with have the protection of God over their personal spirit and usually will not proceed with deliverance unless they can share the salvation experience with us. This is based upon the fact that we would not want to lead an unbeliever into a trap of being possessed by even more unholy spirits (Matthew 12:43-45). His statement also holds that he had to perform, rendering the gospel mute. This change of understanding one's role demonstrates much more than a change in procedure; it highlights one of conviction. The Power of God and His Gospel supersede anything man could ever offer.

The Providential Worldview reportedly holds that God is sovereign and controls everything in the universe which He created. Furthermore, the essence of one's purpose is how one relates to, or chooses not to, relate with God. These statements are not contrary to a Warfare Worldview. In fact, they echo what we have been sharing with you in the previous paragraphs. While God knew beforehand that there would be rebellion on Lucifer's part and that he would take a third of the angels with him, we believe it saddened the Lord that fellowship was broken there. Because God is all powerful, He can work all things for good; and therefore, wickedness is limited in scope. He redeems. We agree that God is in sovereign control of everything; while at the same time, He permits man free will and permits Satan limited rule over the earth for a time. We also agree that one's relationship with God contributes to what happens in the deliverance session.

Jesus cautioned those who followed Him regarding deliverance ministry in Luke 10:20. The admonition was not to abandon deliverance work, but rather it should not be regarded as a place of accomplishment or esteem for us. He encouraged His disciples to value relationship with God over pride and results. He said their delight should be that their names were written in Heaven, i.e. the reason for rejoicing was their relationship with God the Father and inferring that their names were already written in the Lamb's Book of Life (Revelation 20:12, 15).

The crux of the opposing argument as presented in this select article is based on a confession that the author permitted pride to influence his thought patterns leading to the thought that his personal performance in deliverance ministry was of utmost importance. Because he operated from a state of pride, his ability to see that the Warfare Worldview embraces the authority and power of God was obscured. While the illusion portrayed of Satan's Protection Racket which operates much like a gang that requires payment in exchange for protection may have been employed in his sphere of influence, we do not find there is sufficient evidence provided to generalize such a claim.

Again, there are some very bold assumptions presented by the commentator as being held by all those with a Warfare Worldview. For example, the supposition that asserts our hope is not completely in Christ and His resurrection after death. We believe that there is more to his thought process than the commentator shares. He appears to wrestle with how one views our makeup of spiritual being and physical being. One that holds the view that we are only body and soul or dichotomous, could easily be disturbed and misunderstand teaching that is based on the premise that we are truly a three part being: body, soul (mind and emotions), and spirit. As a tripartite being, each personal spirit is completely secure upon asking the Holy Spirit to indwell us at the time of salvation. There is complete deliverance by the work of the cross and resurrection, and thus it is complete deliverance of our eternal spirit by the Gospel.

The troublesome place for some attempting to apply the tripartite teaching in a dichotomous context is that unholy spirits may still have access to our emotions and physical body. For ease of example, just because a habitual smoker or someone addicted to any other number of vices is saved, does that mean they are all immediately free of the compulsion of their individual addiction? No, of course not. Yes, it happens on occasion, but not as a generalized rule. Because of this, those that hold to a two-part being struggle to understand that a Warfare Worldview believes in the sufficiency of Jesus' perfect sacrifice. If you only have two parts, how do you split will and emotion? Are those relegated to our soul or to our physical body? If will and spirit are synonymous, then they can lay claim to a faulty reasoning that the gospel only partially delivers us. We would argue that if you hold fast to a dichotomous being, it is more appropriate to assign the will and emotions to the physical being which permits the enemy an influence rather than possession of a believer's soul.

There also seems to be a blending of prosperity gospel with Warfare Worldview in the presentation of the argument. This again is a separate topic and should be kept so. It is a false belief to equate obedience with ease of life and conversely disobedience with hardship. Jesus said that we are to take up our cross and follow Him (Matthew 10:38, Luke 14:27). That does not indicate a life of ease.

Additionally, this commentator borders on a position that would hold counseling in very low regard. While God is not bound by, nor does He employ a systematic approach for every human being, we believe there is value in presenting varying materials as a way to deal with behaviors and thought patterns. Scripture says we are to encourage and edify each other (Acts 15:30-33, 1 Thessalonians 5:11, 2 Timothy 4:2, Hebrews 3:13). We are also to cry and rejoice with each other (Romans 12:15). We do not ascribe to the theory that counseling is unholy because it may put forth exercises and applications to help one become more Christ-like that were not included in the Scriptures.

In reading the author's thoughts, we question whether or not God's discipline may have come into play. By his own admission, *he* tried everything *he* could think of to make *his* ministry effective which implies the position that human effort is what effects the spiritual change. Is it possible that God permitted the author's call of reaching others for the Kingdom to remain, since one's call is irrevocable (Romans 11:29), but removed the anointing from deliverance ministry because of a manifestation of pride and self-reliance?

He concluded by identifying the key issue as being one's underlying worldview. While our worldview plays a role in our decisions, we would argue that the key issue is the source of our identity. If our identity is as a Child of God, one can operate from a blend of both worldviews as presented in this argument. The fallacy of reasoning against the Warfare Worldview stems from a heart issue that continually asserts man must perform and achieve the victory. This simply is not true. God is the Victor and the victory has already been achieved through His sufficiency and sovereignty, and many believers who hold to a Warfare Worldview hold tightly to this foundational concept.

LEADER'S GUIDE

In addition to using *Behind Enemy Lines* for individual study, the material has also been designed to use in large and small group settings. We are available to present the material as a weekend seminar. Please contact us at info@bluefirelegacy.org to schedule an event.

Alternatively, the book can be used for smaller groups in sessions of varying lengths. Most chapters can be covered in a 90 minute – 2-hour block of time. For shorter meeting times, we suggest dividing chapters by sub-topics.

For the Inner Healing Exercise, it is optional to divide into smaller groups. Please make sure you allow sufficient time and have an adequate number of facilitators present if you choose this method.

You will find group discussion questions which differ from chapter questions below. These are optional. It should be evident where group discussions should take place during the lesson.

WHAT IS SPIRITUAL WARFARE?

What does spiritual warfare mean to you?

Discuss different types of gates and the functions of gates.

SALVATION

What is the difference between our soul and spirit?

Discuss why a split or false identity can affect your spirit as an unbeliever but not as a Believer.

THE ARMOR OF GOD

Discuss the varying types of pads and protective equipment used in sports.

While reviewing the Armor of God, discuss what each piece of armor protects or permits us to do better.

BAPTISM

What do you think about when you hear the word "baptism?"

Discuss the difference between the Holy Spirit coming into a Believer and coming upon them with power.

FORGIVENESS

True or False
* Forgiveness releases the offender of all responsibility and denies there was any wrong done. [False]
* Forgetting is a required element of forgiveness. [False]
* You must fully reconcile as evidence of fully forgiving. [False]

Discuss how we hold ourselves in bondage when we choose not forgive others.

Inner Healing Exercise: If using in a group format, break into smaller groups and do inner healing as appropriate. If possible, the group leader should not facilitate one of the smaller groups, so they can be available for additional assistance as needed.

DOORS, LEGAL RIGHTS, AND STRONGHOLDS

Discuss what vows have been made by individuals in the group.

What are some spiritual strongholds?

BELIEVERS' AUTHORITY IN CHRIST

What authority figures are in your life?

Discuss ways in which we walk in Christ's authority.

PROTECTION AFTER THE BATTLE

What is the purpose of a seal?

Define discipleship.

What are some ways the church can implement discipleship?

How can you disciple others?

WEAPONS AND TECHNIQUES OF WARFARE

Discuss how love is a weapon of warfare.

Discuss the difference between praying and commanding.

HOW SATAN WORKS

What is one way in which Satan attempts to manipulate or trick you? How do you combat that?

Discuss the difference between guilt and conviction.

THE PLAYERS AND SPECIFIC SPIRITS

What are some names of God?

Have you ever seen an angel? Describe how they appeared.

WALKING IN VICTORY

Describe a time when you over-spiritualized a situation.

What is the one thing in this study that has stood out to you the most?

BIBLIOGRAPHY

DeWaay, Bob. "How Deliverance Ministries Lead People to Bondage." *Cicministry.org/commentary/issue78.htm.* September/October 2003. Web. 11 September 2018.

Furious Love Deluxe Edition. Wilson, Darren. "Jan Sjoerd Pasterkamp," "Mattheus van der Steen," DVD. Wanderlust Productions, 2010.

Frangipane, Francis. *The Three Battlegrounds Revised Edition.* Cedar Rapids, IA: Arrow Publications, Inc., 2012.

Holy Ghost Deluxe Edition. Wilson, Darren. "Che Ahn", DVD. Wanderlust Productions, 2014.

Ing, Richard. *Spiritual Warfare.* New Kensington, PA: Whitaker House, 1996.

Jackson, John Paul. *Needless Casualties of War.* Flower Mound, TX: Streams Ministries International, 2013.

Jackson, John Paul. *Unmasking the Jezebel Spirit.* Colleyville, TX: Streams Publishing House, 2002.

Larson, Bob. *Demon Proofing Prayers.* Shippensburg, PA: Destiny Image® Publishers, Inc., 2011.

Simmons, Brian. *The Psalms Poetry on Fire, The Passion Translation.* Racine, WI: BroadStreet Publishing Group, LLC, 2014.

Splankna Therapy Institute. "Baptism Matters." Splankna Therapy Institute Newsletter (Dec. 2012): n. pag. Splankna Institute. E-mail. 25 Dec. 2012.

Tozer, A.W. *The Pursuit of God.* n.p., 1948

Mark and Dallas Henslee established Blue Fire Legacy with a desire to meet the needs of ministers, missionaries, lay leaders, and those seeking to passionately follow Christ. Mark and Dallas offer consultation, counseling support, and speaking engagements.

Please contact us at info@bluefirelegacy.org to schedule an event.

Blue Fire Legacy is a donor funded ministry. To learn more about Blue Fire Legacy, subscribe to our email newsletter, or order additional materials, please visit www.bluefirelegacy.org.

www.ingramcontent.com/pod-product-compliance
Lightning Source LLC
Chambersburg PA
CBHW031140160426
43193CB00008B/204